Routine

Ultimate Daily Routine for More
Energy and Success

*(The Essential Guide to Creating Your Personal
Morning Routine That Will Actually Work)*

Samuel Stokes

Published By **Gautam Kumar**

Samuel Stokes

Routine: Ultimate Daily Routine for More Energy and Success (The Essential Guide to Creating Your Personal Morning Routine That Will Actually Work)

ISBN 978-1-7382957-9-1

Legal & Disclaimer

Table Of Contents

Chapter 1: Routines

Now that we've piqued your interest in the energy of ordinary, it's time to begin small. Overhauling your complete existence in a single fell swoop is a recipe for burnout, so on this financial disaster, we'll recognition on laying a sturdy basis.

The first step is reflecting on your cutting-edge-day conduct. Do you revel in like every day blends into an unstructured haze? Are crucial regions of your life lacking route or consistency? Jot down your reflections without judgment the purpose proper here is genuinely gaining readability.

Next, choose out certainly 2-three exercises you want to interest on setting up. Your morning regular and a everyday paintings everyday are commonly proper starting factors as they've huge-ranging effects. Define while the ordinary will arise every day, how prolonged it will take, and step-with the aid of using way of-step moves. You'll thank yourself later for maintaining it easy at the start.

Some examples of morning exercise that p.C. A effective punch? Waking up half-hour earlier lets in for exercising, relaxation, or planning your day. Having your outfit/lunch organized the night in advance than technique smooth sailing. Mapping out your physical sports on a weekly calendar brings them into your landscape for suitable.

It's additionally critical to design physical video games that healthy your herbal frame clock and lifestyle go along with the flow. Are you a morning person who thrives beginning early Or a night time owl who does their extremely good artwork later? Listen for your strength ranges and accommodate for that reason.

With physical sports in location, live affected person however continual as your new conduct form. Expect u.S.A.And downs as you regulate that's ordinary. Soon, the benefits of shape and formality will have you ever ever

ever addicted to dwelling existence thru using normal.

Reflect to your current behavior and understand regions to beautify

Even describing this technique as "identifying areas to decorate" frames it negatively and putting ourselves up for fulfillment manner maintaining off that attitude. Let's keep in thoughts it rather as gaining belief into wherein we need extra a laugh, success, or go with the flow in our days.

Start with the aid of taking 10-15 minutes with pen and paper (or notes app!) and write down everything you in all likelihood did yesterday from morning to night time time time with out judgment. Now look for styles which responsibilities energized you? When did your recognition begin to flag? Did you rely carefully on self-discipline or caffeine at any issue?

It also can be illuminating to check your calendar/to-do listing apps over the last few weeks. Are exceptional commitments greater draining than others? Do you have got got readability on how and in which you spend discretionary time?

Don't obsess over perceived "troubles" for now. Just phrase objectively. The purpose is to benefit an expertise of methods your modern rhythms serve or limit you so that you can decorate regular stories via thoughtful tweaks.

Routines want to feel like an possibility, no longer an obstacle. So if superb realizations deliver frustration, set them apart for now we'll get to those later in a extra positive mindset. Focus instead on in which your natural strengths and interests lie, so workout routines make bigger who you already are at your splendid.

Choose a ordinary layout that works for your way of life

When it consists of selecting a ordinary layout, one period does now not in form all.

The awesome preference is some issue works harmoniously alongside facet your herbal energy tiers, commitments, and opportunities.

If you thrive on shape, focused every day planners laying out hourly blocks may be your style. Others pick out a free weekly calendar to time table key priorities while leaving wiggle room. Flexible sporting activities work well too middle components like morning pages or motion are everyday, and different factors shift.

Are you a night time time time owl who does modern artwork after darkish? Then backloading your day probably flows higher. Early birds may additionally discover frontloading mornings maximum efficient. If a few days are busier than others, block the ones concurrently for ease.

Also, take into account your circle of relatives! Solo physical activities range from juggling own family goals. Both require compromise and conversation to revel in sustainable for all.

Don't strain about perfection both. Routines evolve with revel in. I suggest beginning barebones virtually 2-three middle behavior then construct from there. Revisit your layout monthly to appearance if tweaks serve you higher.

Most importantly, make sports seamless and coffee-strive. Stack comparable obligations collectively by means of manner of location to experience a lot much less fragmented. Also popularity on entertainment through rituals you want each day, now not chores on my own.

Pick 2-3 routines to start with and keep it smooth

Here is a few advice on selecting your preliminary 2-three sporting events:

Focus on physical video games as a manner to make the most crucial impact with the least attempt. Things like morning and midnight exercising routines frequently in form the invoice, as they set the tone for your complete day.

Be sensible about what you may sustainably located into impact right now without going overboard. Choose exercises you recognize you'll preserve up with without resenting them.

Consider physical activities that lay the foundation for destiny behavior. For instance, beginning a every day planning time makes forming remarkable exercises tons less tough down the road.

Choose workout routines in a single in each of a kind life domains if possible one centered on paintings/productivity, a few other on fitness/self-care. A balanced begin is right.

Build your exercise routines round actions you already do regularly to 3 degree. This makes use of cutting-edge behavioral momentum in choice to beginning truely from scratch.

Collaborate with others if wearing sports include shared household duties. Getting purchase-in from circle of relatives makes physical games jointly supported in region of some exceptional "chore."

Keep exercises clean but impactful. For instance, honestly 15 minutes each day of movement plus a weekly meal plan is greater potential than becoming a member of a boot camp!

Focus first on exercise exercises that energize you instead of feeling like a "have-to." Joyful rituals are maximum probably to stick lengthy-term.

The purpose is development, no longer perfection. Adjust sports based totally on the way you enjoy them in workout every week. Evolution is the call of the sport right here.

Morning Routines

Every new day holds wealthy ability, and your mornings set the colorful tone. This financial ruin busts not unusual myths approximately why mornings remember and gives some of quite powerful routine alternatives.

We'll begin through exploring the concrete technological understanding behind morning rituals. Our bodies have natural circadian rhythms tweaked thru behavior, so movements as diffused as dawn publicity effect metabolism, cognizance, and mood all day. When we energize ourselves in alignment with innate biorhythms, lives redesign results.

From there, keep in thoughts your morning kind earlier than choosing wearing events. Do you need solitude or agency? Calm or stimulation? Options embody:

Early riser: Exercise, mag, meditation. Movement shifts circadian clocks for a long-lasting strain.

Reader: Breakfast while skimming facts, and blogs. Staying curious optimizes traumatic conditions beforehand.

Productivity guru: Plan your day over espresso. Visualize successes to actualize them seamlessly.

Night owl: Gradual start through yoga, and song. Gentle mornings ease the transition for wiser evenings.

Regardless of persona, consistency wins over hobbies by myself. Master exercising workouts requiring five-10 minutes maximum to shape sustainable well-being behavior. Combine morning momentum with afternoon mirrored image for balanced days ahead.

Does one recurring name to you? Experiment strain-unfastened we modify as insights emerge. Your mornings are sacred; deal with them as such via thoughtful ritual. When dealt with with care, each sunrise will become your each day rebirth.

Examples of specially effective morning sports

Here are 3 examples of specifically powerful morning exercises:

The Rise and Reflect Routine

5:30 AM: Wake up and located on workout clothes with music or podcast

5:forty five AM: 30 min outdoor walk/jog/yoga bypass your frame

6:15 AM: Back inner for five min meditation or journaling

6:20 AM: Shower and dress

6:30 AM: Breakfast on the equal time as prepping lunch/coffee for the day

The Early Energy Routine

5:00 AM: Hit snooze till five:15, then awaken with solar lamp

5:15 AM: Make the bed and tidy the room with upbeat song

5:30 AM: 30 min power education exercise

6:00 AM: Shower and dress

6:30 AM: Prep fruit, oats, coffee, and p.C. Lunch

The Night Owl Negotiator

7:00 AM: Wake to calm song, perhaps a five min stretch

7:15 AM: Make tea or coffee and test notifications

7:30 AM: Respond to essential emails from mattress

8:00 AM: Shower and dress for the day

eight:30 AM: Hot breakfast and p.C. Healthy lunch

The key's locating a routine that devices your day up for achievement while although feeling peaceful and sustainable to your life-style. Don't be afraid to test and tweak sports to find out what energizes you each morning.

The significance of starting your day properly set

Here are a few key motives why properly installing your mornings is so critical:

Mornings are even as your self-discipline muscle mass are maximum powerful, so utilizing that attention to shape your day's trajectory pays off massive time. Small moves like preparing lunch/coffee make healthy options less difficult even as disruptions hit midday.

How you start gadgets your brain up neurologically via priming effects. Waking gently in area of frantically has profound affects on strain, attention, and selection-making all day long.

Physical interest inside the AM has number one metabolic perks in choice to evenings like optimizing insulin sensitivity and fats-burning. It additionally yields the "sparkling begin impact" in which momentum carries over actually for productiveness.

Rituals like gratitude journaling or rest prep your mentality for thriving. You rise organized to gather every day's opportunities rather than reacting to superficial pressing noises.

Consistency is prime for regular benefits, so mornings make behavior less difficult because of the truth that willpower is maximum. Forming tremendous beginning patterns lays the foundation for learning exceptional areas of lifestyles.

Relationships flourish while you greet others, yourself blanketed, with warm temperature as opposed to exhaustion. Your humans and work each take advantage of you displaying up certainly gift every dawn.

So whether it's hitting the snooze button or powering through with mindfulness, appreciate your mornings as sacred. How you start affects the whole go together with the go with the flow of your sunrise to sundown.

Chapter 2: Morning Habitual Seamless

Here are some tips for making your morning ordinary seamless:

Prep as a good buy as possible the night earlier than. Have garments/luggage organized, lunch packed, and espresso/breakfast prepped to restrict alternatives.

Automate repetitive duties. Set the alarm, lighting, and coffee maker to show on so your morning starts off evolved itself without strive from you.

Stack workouts with the aid of the use of location. Do associated duties consecutively in place of fragment all over. Example: Shower on the equal time as coffee brews so that you can drink it all through skin care.

Go to mattress early sufficient to experience rested. A greater 30 minutes creates a buffer for sound asleep in slightly or taking element on your regular.

Find a easy transition from bed room. Maybe maintain weights thru your bed for ground bodily sports activities to make it clean to begin shifting right away.

Use calendar invites. Block out ordinary time with reminders to honor that point and keep away from double reserving.

Have backups for wrinkles. Alternate breakfast alternatives or meditations prevent feeling caught if a ordinary object runs out.

Don't be difficult on yourself. Consistency topics extra than perfection. When life interrupts, seamlessly adapt and maintain the momentum going.

The reason is flow, now not fuss. With a few tweaks, your mornings can autonomously set you up to shine each day! Experiment pressure-free.

Daily Work Routines

Now that you've mastered getting your personal lifestyles dealt with effortlessly every morning, it's time to apply those same principles to optimize your workdays. Whether you're employed, freelance, or juggling every, keeping ordinary art work rhythms will take your output to the following level. Our jobs have a number one have an effect on on intellectual nicely-being too even as approached ritualistically, art work will become its ceremony of contribution.

The structure is high, however pressure breeds stagnancy. The proper sporting events streamline your efforts toward herbal popularity durations at the identical time as safeguarding flexibility. Work ebbs and flows every day, so we need to conform. Think plenty less like a tightly wound clock and more like the tides regular but bending gracefully with situation.

There are three pillars to recall in delineating your best workflow: time management, bodily preparations, and mind-set. Let's have a observe each to craft physical activities that empower you with every productiveness and simplicity.

Time control starts offevolved offevolved with putting smooth, calendar-blocked obstacles spherical art work hours. Are you a person who dreams a sharp nine-five or is flexibility essential to your rhythm? Either manner, statistics your expert span calms obsessiveness round obligations. For most, 7-four permits mid-days quite distraction-loose on the same time as respecting electricity dips because the sun devices.

Within the ones hours, designate periods 25-50 mins for dedicated consciousness on a top to-do observed thru 5-15 minutes of rest. Brief breaks each 90 minutes revitalize our depleted prefrontal cortices answerable for excessive-degree questioning. Multitasking sabotages finishing touch with the useful resource of using diluting attention great to tackle one great aspect at a time.

For time-blockading templates adaptable to every day ebbs, attempt the well-known

Pomodoro technique of 25 minutes on/5 mins off or maybe 90/30 intervals for huge responsibilities. Apps like Toggl and DeskTime help track your beats too. Just switching contexts enables our minds live engaged in which boredom can also otherwise creep in.

And don't neglect approximately the gift of open location in your ordinary. Having time deliberately set apart every day to assume, brainstorm, or permit the muse wander untethered lets in your amazing thoughts to germinate. Creativity thrives on the point of chaos, so don't overstructure mission each.

With time manipulate outlining the skeleton of your go together with the glide, physical arrangements flesh it out pretty without a doubt. Designating your handiest paintings zones at domestic is going a ways. For example, studies show that sincerely popularity periodically boosts cognitive characteristic thru 25% possibly you stand at a tall kitchen island or bar to combine it up.

Ergonomics are the entirety proper right here. Craft areas tailor-made on your posture with adjustable desks and balance balls if seated extended-term. Proper lights, minimal distractions, and cushty aesthetics promote smooth cognizance. Noise-canceling headphones or white noise tunes out interruptions peacefully. Movement is motivation too upward push up with reminder alarms or bookmark favorite taking walks meetings.

At the office, employ your surroundings with purpose. Break out collaboration schooling to conference rooms in vicinity of suffocating underneath open floor plans. Commune casually with colleagues over espresso on muddle-loose dwelling room couches. Adjust temperature and natural lighting if possible our primal brains are even though activated through such diffused influences over overall performance. Consider repute desks or custom designed nameplates to customise otherwise standard cubicles. Crafting sanctuary even in stark regions uplifts our paintings soul.

Finally, the inner maximum alternate occurs in attitude. Cultivating compassion for your self and others transforms any hobby into a conduit for contribution in preference to drudgery. Notice coworkers' humanity beyond obligations offer useful useful resource freely thru lively listening or small gestures of care. Leading with care lightens definitely anybody's load whilst bringing out their quality.

Shift internal narratives too. Rather than disturbing urgency, exhale right into a focused presence in every 2d. See barriers as fascinating puzzles stimulating creativity as opposed to frustration. Focus on analyzing, no longer notable consequences. Notice fulfillment via development, no longer particular achievements by myself. This softer attitude sustains career sturdiness via tough seasons.

It's everyday to ebb motivationally as electricity wanes deliberate rewards like exercise, social dates, or pastimes on the horizon refuel. Make your non-work self without a doubt as valued to save you burnout. Nourishing wellbeing from dawn to nightfall holistically influences normal usual overall performance too. Have compassion for imperfect days, forgive your self freely, and keep at your craft with staying electricity. Eventually recurring becomes 2nd nature a springboard on your wonderful contributions.

By thoughtfully designing your day, You claim location to professionalize your paintings on the identical time as securing alignment collectively collectively together with your values and properly-being. This synergy is the sanctuary we are searching for waft emerging from association in desire to electricity of will. Routines need to experience an entire lot less constrictive than expressive of our real rhythms. Achieving paintings-life concord starts from within, but smooth rituals useful resource maintaining that insight near each day.

With these pillars of time, location, and angle in thoughts, strive out some templates over the subsequent weeks:

The Minimalist:

7:30-12:30 PM Focus mode at home with 25-minute durations and mid-morning walk.

12:30-1:30 PM Prepared lunch on the kitchen counter while catching up on people.

1:30-4:30 PM Focus mode another time with a committed brainstorming period at three.

4:30-five PM Wrap up and begin shutdown recurring.

The Creator:

September 11 AM Focus on smaller to-do's at domestic desk with reputation alternatives.

11-12 PM Outdoor stroll + brainstorm new thoughts at the drift.

12-1:30 PM Collab conferences at a close-by espresso maintain for perception.

1:30-four PM Deep recognition time on center initiatives with 30-minute periods.

4-five:30 PM Flex time on your selected co-art work area for tinkering.

The Mentor:

7:30-9 AM Focus at domestic on private responsibilities.

nine-10 AM Morning standup meeting with the resource of video call.

10-12 PM 1:1 mentee check-ins and challenge evaluations.

12-1 PM Mentor chat over shared lunch ruin.

1-3 PM Core obligations at a standing desk in a personal workplace.

three-four PM Networking espresso and quick mentee wrap-ups.

Notice which days go with the flow exceptional and don't pressure inflexible adherence regulate templates weekly as desired. Building routines with room to flex serves you prolonged-term. Your perfect workflow awaits discovery via playful trial and determination for your properly-being.

Exercise & Nutrition Routines

People frequently forget exercising and vitamins as certifiable physical games of their personal right. Yet our properly being relies upon significantly on the ones each day disciplines for easy sailing lengthy-time period. Irregular fitness leaves us like flashlights walking low, each day out of hobby a touch dimmer with out replenishing ourselves properly. Nourishment forms the coal powering our engine, so why shirk sports tending to it intentionally?

This bankruptcy delves into laying strong exercise and consuming foundations addiction thru valuable dependancy. We'll begin by means of analyzing motivators like feeling, characteristic, and amusement as drivers beyond aesthetic whims a sustainable thoughts-set empowers lengthy-haul safety. Flexibility and adaptability also are paramount right here to provide grace on imperfect days. Routines serve us; we don't serve stress by myself.

First up is exercise for thoughts-frame equilibrium. Many expect jogging out calls for devoted hours, but steady 5-10 minute periods suit more realistically into lifestyles's ebb and waft at the same time as yielding advantages. Try the Nike Training Club app for study-along workouts of all intensities from yoga to boxing fun, motivating, and loose! Whatever sports activities in form your spirit, time table them unapologetically.

Whether at home, gymnasium, or outside, having a bendy weekly template will increase the probabilities of sticking to an exercise habitual. For instance, Mon/Wed/Fri do a HIIT circuit that specialize in electricity. Tues/Thurs float for a 30-minute stroll, run or hike tapping cardio. Weekends lend to longer classes of a favorite pastime or rest if wanted. Playing with workout orders the usage of an app like Freeletics customizes your routine similarly at the same time as easing boredom.

What's maximum important is movement turning into a essential, non-negotiable day by day thread stretching your frame in some style even though most effective a short everyday. Strong workout routines equal adaptation and resilience over stresses inside the mind too. Just listening to what serves you prevents burnout. Exercise need to constantly enjoy like nourishment rather than a chore.

On to sustainable ingesting styles focusing greater on fitness than weight by myself. Centering nutrients round whole elements really drives balance prolonged-time period. Keeping shares of pantry/freezer fundamentals like nuts, seeds, canned beans, and lentils ensures short meal guide finally of busy times. Meal prep on weekends prevents frenzied takeout and saves money too.

Try rotating thru the produce of the week as suggestion for current recipes this season maybe kale sautéed with garlic or roasted Brussels sprouts. Pair with a protein like lentils, chook, or salmon plus grains like farro or quinoa. Add spices and sauces freely in keeping with flavor who says healthful needs to be bland? Variety prevents feelings of deprivation that sabotage consistency.

Snacking needn't be an afterthought each complex carbs and fiber hold us entire among meals. Some options: fruit with peanut/almond butter, roasted chickpeas, hummus with veggies, or a homemade strength ball recipe. Factor afternoon snacks intentionally into your regular to prevent impulse alternatives from derailing conduct.

Having constant food and consuming times offers shape allowing your frame's organic rhythms to locate homeostasis. Aim for balanced plates shielding all macronutrients, then allow meals come and cross seasonally with out pressuring any "fine" food regimen. Ultimately it's sustainability via enjoyment, not pressure that changes nicely-being conduct for appropriate.

To help easy your weekly transitions round those exercises, proper here are a few pointers:

Grocery store on Sundays to prep cooking domestic machine for the week in advance. This makes a balanced breakfast/lunch/dinner sequence seamless.

Use a food scale to precisely element recipes for repeatability vs guesswork. Accuracy prevents binges through unintended overeating.

Schedule social workout sports like sports activities sports activities league nights or trekking meetups to sit up for. Togetherness will increase duty deliciously.

Keep exercise garments/footwear seen thru the door or packed for spontaneity anywhere you're that day. Out of sight is out of thoughts for physical activities.

Try activity trackers to begin with for perception vs obsession over numbers 80/20 rule for development, no longer perfection.

Hydrate nightly inventorying pantry naked spots for one-prevent purchasing for normal overall performance.

Rotate amongst exceptional sports activities and recipes month-to-month to keep away from boredom on the equal time as putting in lifelong healthy patterns.

Try experimenting with the templates beneath usually for two weeks before adjusting as needed to your natural rhythms. Refinement honors in which you're at be affected person via the way. Over time habitual will become second nature.

The key's embracing alternate as an evolution in preference to a vacation spot We often lose footing even as picturing transformation as some mountainous top the ones bring about burnout from immoderate striving on my own. Instead, envision your fitness adventure as a flowing river usually discovering itself. With this lens, come to exercises without rigid expectancies that set you as lots as fail from human imperfection.

Progress takes vicinity via constant small wins referred to with appreciation, not in a single day epiphanies. For example, sticking with a exercise ordinary eighty% of the time builds extra wholesome momentum than aiming for a hundred% perfection out of the gate. Approaching exercises from humility and care of self instead of harsh opinions maintain lasting achievement thru nourishing well being from the indoors out.

Having help lights the manner Find properly matched ordinary buddies who keep every outstanding accountable through sharing goals and celebrating small victories collectively. Doing workouts at domestic or the health club is greater fun spontaneously dancing with pals in area of lonesome lifting.

Even digital groups on line instill comradery, as social media thought from others staying devoted motivates our personal endured willpower.

Identify what serves your strength stages and manner of lifestyles then dedicate in fact. Rigidity frequently backfires at the same time as sports struggle with our natural biorhythms or schedules. Listen for what energizes you intrinsically as opposed to strict diets/regimens designed for one-of-a-type temperaments. One individual's HIIT is any other's gentler yoga waft play right right here to tune in actually. Commit completely to your custom designed approach tailor-made to who you're.

Instead of restrictions, body healthy physical games absolutely round consisting of nourishing each day rituals like sure actions or antioxidant-dense produce versus punitive subtraction of "terrible" meals. Indulgences want to return from a place of satiation now not deprivation moderation feels sustainable lengthy-term. Meal prepping and retaining simple healthy staples handy deters binging something as Plan B.

Habits require cues in the environment to paste. Place exercise garments the front and center as a reminder or set each day calendar reminders on your recurring time. Keep wholesome snacks seen and pre-portioned for capture-and-pass ease at the equal time as starvation moves. Diffusing critical oils or lighting fixtures candles makes wholesome meal prepping as hundreds a sensorial enjoy as a chore. Our environment both encourage or discourage continuous adherence to wellness disciplines.

Chapter 3: Elements of A Healthy Meal Prep Ordinary

While spontaneous cooking has its location, incorporating ordinary meal prep into your lifestyle sports elevates nutrients and nicely-being substantially. Advanced making plans is high for regular, balanced home cooking amid anxious schedules. Taking just a few hours on weekends to batch hearty, nutrient-dense food aids the whole week seamlessly.

Let's explore a few center elements to craft your culinary rituals: the whilst, what, and the way of crafting dietary cornerstones helping health each day. With the proper foundations in region, getting ready your fuel feels heaps less chore and greater foxy self-care via taste. After all, nutrients extracted at once from Earth herself set us up for smooth sailing.

Arguably the most essential aspect is choosing an highest wonderful prep day and devoted kitchen window. Sundays generally generally tend excellent after interest unwinding with a complete week's template laid out. Others select combining obligations midday Saturday among errands for shorter weekday stretches. Listen inner on your ideal workflow possibly the morning man or woman deserves weekday preps instead.

Block an uninterrupted 2-4 hour window respecting your prep float. Clear cluttered surfaces, do any knife talents exercising, then play energizing podcasts or tunes to set the mood lightheartedly. Consider grabbing close to buddies for commercial enterprise organization and culinary camaraderie sharing nourishing is self-care in itself! With workouts comes pride while honoring our technique patiently.

Next up is stocking pantry fundamentals making sure healthful variety at a few stage within the week. Keep things flexible exploring seasonal produce at your preferred market. Having stocks of protein like beans, lentils, eggs, and yogurt gives building blocks for countless alternatives. Plus comfort meals like frozen veggies save you excuses for takeout. Simply roasting a sweet potato preserves vitamins far past its smooth shelf existence too.

Get present day by using manner of browsing recipe web websites and cookbooks for inspiration rather than strictly following lists. Look for recipes without problem scalable by way of numerous servings portions for unique meal arrangements. Focus on balancing macros with out dogma probable a grain, inexperienced, and bean framework allowing endless seasonal substitutes. Play with flavor profiles transferring amongst ethnic influences each week for the variety your body craves.

Now onto the delightful how! First cope with dry goods assembly like selfmade granolas, roasted nuts, or electricity bites portioned for snacking within the course of your week. These cunning obligations require much less lively time than cooking entire meals and upload range. For larger dishes, harm it into intuitive tiers protein and veg prep, sauce/marinade prep, after which assembly. Cook dry additives like grains first in bulk for a couple of recipes.

Most critical is batch cooking protein and roasted root veggie staples without trouble repurposed over days. For instance, roast enough chook breasts one night time for tacos, topped salad, and soup later inside the week. Consider one-pot wonders you may set and overlook like soups, chilis, and curries preserving dish cleansing time.

Finally, detail and properly hold dishes to avoid waste. Glassware lets in visualization preventing forgotten leftovers from languishing. Label packing containers certainly with contents and dates for smooth retrieval for the duration of busy days. Freezing 1/2 of of lets in flexibility reheating as hunger hits over two weeks while maintaining nutrients from scratch.

To make maintaining your routine handy, proper right here are some more guidelines:

Prep assembly stations by using manner of way of detail proteins right right here, grains there, for a easy workflow.

Use templates to without issue duplicate successful recipes adapting flavors seasonally.

Involve kids hands-on for education and buy-in schooling lifestyles abilties.

Prep easy food for rushed nights leaving little room for takeout excuses.

Store elements through manner of use-via dates first in, first out for freshness.

Strategies for making exercise and weight loss program modifications stick

Here are sample weekly exercise sports activities for one among a kind health stages that will help you discover your float and gather consistency in a sustainable but effective way:

Beginner Level:

The intention is building preferred mobility, and easy energy, and installing an workout dependancy.

Mon: 30 min Walk/Jog Start with on foot intervals incorporating short 30 sec jogs to heat up and ease into motion.

Tues: Yoga Flow Follow on-line 20-minute novice yoga video specializing in stretching and important poses.

Wed: 30 min Walk/Jog Gradually increase jog periods over weeks as snug.

Thurs: Light Bodyweight Circuit Do each workout like squats, pushups, and lunges for 30 sec with 30-sec rest among for 10 mins.

Fri: Rest Active rest day like moderate stretching is normally recommended.

Sat: 30 min Bike Ride Opt for flat community trails maintaining a informal tempo.

Sun: Rest or Light Activity Gentle yoga, stretching, or a in addition 30-minute stroll.

Intermediate Level:

The intention is to construct power, muscle tone, and aerobic staying power via numerous stressful conditions.

Mon: HIIT Circuit Do a combination of sporting events like squats, lunges, pushups, and abs in brief rounds of 30-2nd paintings/30-2d relaxation for 20 mins.

Tues: Outdoor Sports Meet pals for pickup football, tennis, and hiking for 45-60 mins.

Wed: Strength Training Focus on compound moves like deadlifts, rows, and presses with dumbbells or body weight for 30-forty five mins.

Thurs: Rest Active healing like foam rolling is normally advocated.

Fri: Dance or Boxing Class Group exercise gives motivation and range.

Sat: Long Bike Ride Gradually increase distances on trails over weeks.

Sun: Yoga Commit to 60 min vinyasa or yin exercising deepening poses.

Advanced Level:

The goal is universal performance optimization through excessive but balanced training.

Mon: Cross Training Circuit of 8-10 excessive bodily video games from walking to swimming with minimum rest.

Tues: Strength Heavy weightlifting specializing in 3-5 physical games regular with body element for forty five-60 minutes.

Wed: Rest Stretching, meditation, or slight aerobic encouraged.

Thurs: Stamina Long run, motorbike, or athletic talent workout over 60-90 mins.

Fri: HIIT 5 rounds of high-depth body weight or device carrying occasions for 20 minutes.

Sat: Sports Commit to close by means of entertainment league or event.

Sun: Active Recovery Gentle yoga, stretches, or walks emphasizing mobility.

Adapt schedules as wished primarily based totally on converting energies, injuries, or existence occasions. Consistency and taking note of your body are keys to maintaining development thoroughly over the years. I desire this form of templates sparks your next exciting glide

Schedule flexibility and self-care

One of the top motives humans give up on building exercises is that lifestyles necessarily throws curveballs busy periods at paintings, appointments that run late, wonder visitors, ailments, tour days, own family obligations, and additional. These unpredictable disruptions can revel in like ordinary disasters, inflicting us to toss the entire gadget apart in frustration. However, with a piece of pliability and foresight baked into your planning, you can maintain consistency and progress even on off-kilter days.

The first step is constructing backup and opportunity alternatives without delay into your sporting events. For instance, if commuting time is variable, have bendy begin and quit times in your morning ordinary in desire to a inflexible clock time table. If exercise appears one-of-a-kind on high-quality days, plan exchange sports activities activities that could seamlessly fill that ordinary's not unusual time slot. Having a "plan B" and "plan C" situation mentioned minimizes scrambling on the same time as changes are wanted.

Another method is batching sports. For example, do you have were given artwork conferences scheduled decrease lower again-to-lower once more a few mornings that week? Consider combining your bathe, morning pages, and powerful playlist with the useful resource of way of doing them right away after waking as an awful lot as unfastened up uninterrupted blocks later. Or package all emails and prep art work into one chew in case you recognize you'll be out of the place of business at noon on fantastic days. Batching is efficient and allows you to keep entire sporting activities ordinary with intentionally scheduled activities.

Advanced guidance techniques like meal planning and outfit layouts similarly lessen nighttime and morning choice fatigue. Do you prep substances on Sunday so healthy dinners come collectively rapid throughout the week? Pack lunches the night time time in advance than? Have gym garments ready to move through the door? Minor scheduling extra workdays however yield important pressure consolation at the same time as moments are unpredictable.

Part of recurring fulfillment includes fostering an mind-set of flexibility everywhere possible. Remember the ones systems exist to serve you, not rule you. If a ordinary genuinely isn't sensible every now and then, allow yourself to modify with out self-grievance. Feel confident that sticking to the middle necessities 80% of the time despite the fact that yields brilliant blessings, and your efforts will common out over time as life settles into new rhythms.

Some days may allow room for simplest a stripped-down mini-regular. That's flawlessly extremely good! Consistency is keeping the underlying purpose and interest regions in desire to following sporting activities mechanically regardless of practicality. For instance, if mornings are jam-packed, spend 5 targeted mins writing in your journal and eating a wholesome breakfast on the flow in place of a greater complicated ordinary. Quality topics extra than sheer amount.

Speaking of exceptional, strive shifting your mindset from exercises being a task listing to habits being instances for nurturing your self. Reframe interruptions or modifications now not as failures however as life occasions to workout bendy questioning and prioritizing self-care. For instance, in case you entice a cold, spend that habitual's scheduled workout duration sipping tea with a ebook in a heat tub instead. Respond to disruptions by the use of doubling down on kindness and nourishment.

Enlist responsibility buddies to check in on every different's regular improvement and problem-remedy disruptions together. Brainstorming with others generates extra solutions than worrying by myself. Not best does teamwork lessen isolation, but discussing habitual setbacks in an answer-centered way trains our important inner voice to be compassionate in place of harshly self-judgmental over perceived "lapses."

Finally, use era responsibly to your benefit. Digital calendars allow colour-coding sporting events so busy periods stand out earlier of time for adjustment making plans. Fitness trackers and dependancy-building apps hold sports top-of-thoughts with periodic notifications and encourage endurance thru check-ins and aim-putting. Pre-populated calorie and macro-counting food ease nutritional workouts. Automated recurring duties like invoice pay or economic financial savings transfers appear seamlessly in the history.

Chapter 4: Adding Nurturing Sports Activities For Rest

By now you've installed baseline routines like morning rituals, exercise conduct, and meal prep that preserve you inexperienced. But real stability goes deeper we need to prioritize restoring depleted frightened structures honestly as devotedly as maximizing output. Nurturing restorative wearing activities in shape seamlessly right right right into a full schedule and are every bit as vital for health as nutrients or art work conduct. Let's discover research-sponsored techniques for mindfully unwinding and recharging your batteries.

Start with the useful resource of way of auditing your sleep recurring and surroundings. Most American adults are chronically sleep disadvantaged, which wrecks well-being over time. Establish rituals like putting gadgets away an hour in advance than mattress, the usage of lavender or calming apps to relax your parasympathetic disturbing tool, and setting your mattress room up completely for relaxation. Darkness and cooling temperatures optimize melatonin and deep REM cycles for recovery.

Nature exposes us to daytime and greenery that relieve every day strains. Schedule sun salutations like morning walks soaked in Vitamin D or weeknight stargazing intervals to reboot your outlook via awe and appreciation for lifestyles's clean presents. A experience of connection to the natural worldwide out of doors lends perspective and replenishes our overtaxed fight-or-flight systems.

Many prioritize productiveness to keep away from ugly thoughts and emotions. But avoidance subsequently backfires as unresolved lines appear bodily or psychologically. Carving out time for mindfulness practices offers highbrow immunity through publicity and elegance of existence's difficult terrain with out judgment. Even beginning with five-minute each day meditations cultivates a skillset for regulating emotions and processing life's modifications healthily.

No one enjoys feeling depleted or confused without remedy. Yet relaxation is simply too frequently canceled first while responsibilities loom. Implement relaxation day rituals like mild yoga instructions, artwork journaling or mandala coloring, Epsom salt baths with audiobooks, and whole30-fashion food. Give your entire thoughts-frame device permission and tool to get higher with out hustling via exhaustion. This fuels your reserves to then show up absolutely for responsibilities with sustainable electricity and focus.

Does your love language encompass outstanding time? Foster rejuvenating relationships by means of proscribing or enhancing display show time to be completely gift without distraction. Make deep listening with out recommendation-giving a latest relationship competencies thru sports like strolling labs or board games nights. Witnessing and enhancing intimacy among you and cherished ones uplifts every spirit and immune characteristic in this demanding worldwide.

While interests and interests deliver leisure, chasing constant stimulation can backfire into shallow indulgence in preference to mindfulness. Try incorporating lightly stimulating, revolutionary, or altruistic sports into ordinary exercises that align deeply in conjunction with your values and encourage go along with the waft states of popularity without pressure or guilt like crafting, studying an device, studying, or volunteering in small doses. Striking this balance nourishes your revel in of reason.

Unclench and launch anxiety saved at some point of your body with restorative yoga nidra sleep visualizations, a laugh song, or strength art work like reiki, acupressure, rubdown, or craniosacral treatment. Notice in that you physical deliver strain on your body and establish rituals to consciously unwind gotten smaller muscular tissues and mindlessly calm your parasympathetic demanding device so it can relaxation and digest fully each night time time main to revitalization.

Some research hyperlink blue slight wavelengths emitted from devices to disrupted circadian clocks and melatonin suppression. Reduce disrupting tech time inner multiple hours of bed to optimize restorative deep sleep ranges critical for immune characteristic, mobile repair, and reminiscence consolidation. Dim ambient lighting or use a laugh amber-coloured bulbs after dusk.

Commute times are frequently wasted but represent a incredible chew of our days. Use adventure periods creatively for audio recordings of records talks, meditative song, or podcasts that improve on the equal time as sparing brainpower for centered sports activities. This moreover prevents speeding out the door frazzled or arriving home burnt out each counterproductive for unwinding.

Every mobile in our our our our bodies regenerates through the years. Yet our lifestyles regularly lack restorative region for renewal, foremost to advanced getting old, oxidative stress, and contamination. Weekly self-care rituals assist you press highbrow and natural reset buttons: strolls with nature journaling, facials or massages even as budgets allow, lengthy enjoyable baths, luxurious cocoa, and nap time. Embrace your innate human want for restoration as a want in place of frivolous indulgence.

When minor issues improve into whole-blown burnout, drastic measures are had to salvage properly-being and productiveness lengthy-term. Schedule extended holidays or sabbaticals while renewal feels dire, in spite of the fact that inconvenient to begin with. Doing a first rate deal less (in brief or absolutely reducing obligations while preferred thru reevaluation or outsourcing) permits "doing more" as your top notch self sustainably. Protecting non-negotiable relaxation intervals will become a necessity in choice to a power of mind battle.

Some who struggle with pressure or responsibilities can also fear prioritizing self-care signs weakness or indulgence. Reframe it as an alternative as proactive preventative safety on your maximum valued asset your self.

Tracking Progress and Maintaining Motivation

While physical games provide amazing advantages, preserving consistency however calls for energy of mind. No matter wide variety how well-intentioned, self-discipline by myself frequently falls quick at the same time as competing commitments rise up. That's why sustainable responsibility techniques play a key characteristic in lengthy-term recurring success. Let's find out studies-sponsored techniques for retaining your self invested and focused thru inevitable u.S.And downs.

First, getting easy for your "why" subjects immensely. Write a non-public mission announcement detailing precisely why fine carrying activities decorate your nicely-being and values. Refer again while motivation wavers to re-light purpose and defend towards boredom derailing development. Post seen reminders in which you'll see them each day as non-negotiable priorities.

Another powerful tool is enlisting assist structures. Find responsibility companions pursuing similar desires to check in regularly, transfer trade habitual thoughts at the same time as existence changes, and help each other problem-treatment boundaries compassionately. You can also create on line forums, groups, or apps to stay inspired through shared struggles. Feeling answerable for others sustains study-via.

Equally impactful is placing measurable short and lengthy-time period desires that experience as it should be difficult however workable along with your recurring framework. For example, if every day exercise is the motive, chart weekly mileage or length dreams and praise benchmarks. Periodically revisiting targets to make certain they encourage motivation in area of feeling no longer feasible and demotivating.

Taking ordinary "previews" thru following components of your new device even in advance than completely imposing them lets in experimenting without stress, enables troubleshoot demanding situations early on, and builds subconscious momentum earlier than diving all in. Easing into exercises with child steps breeds enthusiasm as opposed to deprivation mindsets that bring about short burnout.

Transparency is a few exclusive underutilized tool. Share your commitments and development publicly to internalize the identification of someone who follows via. Family and social obligation shape healthful behavior of openness whilst letting others cheerlead your victories. Posting workouts, reflections, and consequences sell intrinsic pleasure in consistency through the years that outweighs apprehensions.

Linking exercises and behavior to fabric rewards trains your mind's motivation pathways. Whether rewards are small luxuries like attempting a modern-day eating place after a month of exercise dreams or upgrading machine upon important milestones, allocating a financial value reinforces the link among actions, achievements, and enjoyment. Start small and segment rewards out little by little as workouts become intrinsically profitable.

Journals additionally art work wonders. Regularly documenting sporting sports, feelings, distractions, successes, and setbacks improves meta-interest of patterns affecting consistency in desire to blindly repeating cycles. Look for problems to improve strengths or adjust inclined regions proactively instead of reactively scrambling whilst lapses occur. Tracking development through the years fuels motivation.

Another tactic is getting ritualistic via workout exercises. Certain traditions like celebrating accomplishments shared among pals and circle of relatives foster obligation. Think brunches upon milestone birthdays or dates to speak approximately the beyond period and desires revised as a give up result. Ritualizing routines as a communal addiction strengthens obligation to extra than definitely you on my own over the lengthy haul.

Chapter 5: Tools to Diploma Physical Activities

While willpower and perseverance are critical for recurring achievement, it's also crucial to widely known development along the manner. Taking periodic "test-ins" to degree consequences over weeks or months continues you invested, induced, and focused on non-prevent improvement. Celebrating tough-earned victories renews enthusiasm to hold building wholesome behavior. Let's discover tangible but laugh techniques for tracking modifications and honoring achievements huge and small.

Planning recurring test-ins for your calendar respects your determination through the usage of allocating dedicated reflective time. Whether weekly, biweekly, or monthly, pencil in 30 minutes with journals/notes from that length to be conscious problem topics, accumulate facts, and adjust plans due to this in preference to forgetting till you're "at the back of." Consistency proper right here fosters habitual consistency.

Some prefer to visually positioned up regular checklists by way of their bed or workspace as each day reminders. Marking off finished responsibilities each night or crossing off weekly to-dos on Sundays gives instantaneous dopamine hits and a clear photo of your grit and improvement worthwhile your area. It's a reminder of why sporting activities useful aid fulfillment versus being a nuisance.

Digital gadget deliver size comfort. Apps like Streaks, Routinery, HabitBull, or customized spreadsheets allow logging exercises, assigning issue structures, and tracking modifications in easy visuals over time. Noticing patterns well-known which regions want tweaks or reinforcements a great deal less tough than indistinct reminiscence on my own. Data conjures up you beforehand.

Physical markers additionally can be memorable. Consider commemorating benchmarks via symbols meaningful to you for example, a sticker on your water bottle each week you hit hydration desires, stringing beads on a bracelet for days you journaled, or putting "x" huge fashion of cash in a jar in keeping with experience with pals or circle of relatives each month spent strengthening the ones bonds. The rituals engage your senses for deeper duty.

Many wearing events absolutely invite quantitative statistics tracking for only health. Fitness apps or wearable tech make charting workout workout routines, steps, coronary heart charge variability, or sleep over weeks 2nd nature. Reviewing development charts from a bird's-eye view additives satisfaction from seen proof of strive and staying power paying dividends over the years you may now not feel inside the conflict of every day wearing sports on my own.

Celebrating tough-gained routine milestones boosts morale to head subsequent thresholds. Plan capability victories from the outset, whether or not or not it's trying a brand new recipe after sticking to nutrients physical games for two weeks or profitable finishing a months-prolonged monetary monetary savings goal with a completely specific enjoy. Pile small rewards at some stage in similarly to improvement markers a modern day tea for hitting every day meditation time or favored snacks upon workout goals as an example.

Social victories upload achievement. Share regular updates with like-minded pals and own family to encourage every other through every trials and triumphs with potluck celebrations or opinions shared. Building a community round shared commitments strengthens your "why" thru together bearing witness to every different's adjustments and bolstered try.

More good sized rewards help larger milestones revel in momentous in place of normal. Saving for opinions fosters more purchase-in than fleeting treats. Think weekend getaways upon six months of healthful exercising routines or donating to motives reflecting your values after a calendar

365 days of consistency. Major rewards ought to uplift your spirit past quick-term indulgence.

Finally, honor subtle internal adjustments as lots as out of doors outcomes. Make space to have fun extra ease dealing with demanding durations, clearer thinking, stronger relationships or definitely feeling greater aligned day by day thru the way of setting up sports. Small every day gratitude rituals remind us why consistency remains worthwhile via stressful conditions through keeping development the the the front-of-mind. Your well-being deserves acknowledgment!

Strategies for buying lower back on the right music when lifestyles throws curveballs

Despite our nice efforts, life necessarily throws us curves that knock wearing activities askew. Illnesses, adventure weeks, circle of relatives emergencies, or intervals of excessive workload seem without phrase. While disruptions experience discouraging, getting sidelined speedy doesn't define your willpower. What's maximum critical is the way you reply with staying electricity, problem-fixing, and a plan to seamlessly reignite consistency. Let's discover techniques for gracefully deciding on carrying sports once more up after unexpected interruptions.

First, be given that bumps take region with out berating yourself. Perfectionism backfires; behavior require flexibility. Reframe interruptions now not as screw ups however as possibilities to enhance your resilience muscle over the long haul. Once stabilized, decide to resuming sports without delay in location of languishing in what-ifs that lengthen stagnation needlessly.

Rather than reactive scrambling, proactively assume functionality interruptions via contingency making plans. For instance, batch exercises earlier of anticipated busy periods or opportunity options prepared for not unusual disruptions like infection. By creatively leveraging scheduling flexibility built into exercising workouts, disruptions experience much less defeating.

With phrase of drawing close adjustments, ruin massive physical activities into bite-sized mini-behavior to although make ordinary progress. For example, if traveling, decide to journaling just 3 gratitudes each day instead of a complete mirrored image. Little is better than not something; piecemeal participation sidelines inertia till whole physical games smoothly resume.

When thrown primary curveballs like illnesses annoying whole rest, determine to grade by grade easing lower returned into movement once recovered as opposed to harsh expectations. Incorporate restorative self-care sports activities to align along with your capacities slowly increasing as you heal in place of crush-scary regression. Build up robust routines.

Enlist pals to stroll alongside abnormal intervals offering encouragement versus harsh evaluation that sabotages self-efficacy needed to get higher. Their compassion spares dangerous internal complaint of perceived defects or beyond errors that obstruct motivation to restart new leaves.

Mark your resumed workout routines' recommencement date prominently to relaunch with planned rite and the clean highbrow slate of a brand new bankruptcy. Refreshing cause serves renewal higher than brooding in what-changed into. Let that date constitute your persevering determination in vicinity of "days out of place" that breed disgrace counterproductive for restarting robust.

When interruptions strike, use the disruption duration for analyzing as opposed to castigation. Reflect simply on education round prevention, flexibility, and priorities for the subsequent strange spell without self-blame. Insights provide a boost to sports' foundation for weathering upcoming storms higher equipped. Past upsets electricity destiny stability via information.

Most importantly, meet yourself with staying energy as workouts re-root. Weeks can also moreover pass adjusting amid lifestyles's complexities in advance than strong consistency certainly blossoms anew. Trust the herbal ebb and go along with the glide; nurturing soil and consistent tending domesticate hardiness over punishing weeds. You've had been given this allow steady development, no longer perfection be your pal on the journey home to healthful conduct.

Chapter 6: The Grand Tapestry of Lifestyles

We are all, in a single manner or a few different, creatures of recurring. The term "Creature of Routine" refers to a person who finds comfort, performance, and which means that that within the predictability of each day behavior and rituals.

Definition of a "Creature of Routine"

A "Creature of Routine" isn't always absolutely a term, however a manner of lifestyles. It is an

Embodiment of the human tendency to searching for form, order, and familiarity inside the chaos of life this creature thrives on regularity, finding solace within the rhythm of repeated movements and the predictability of everyday life.

The "Creature of Routine" isn't always certain with the beneficial resource of its behavior however liberated thru them.

In the following chapters, we will delve deeper into the location of the "Creature of Routine". We will find out the technological know-how inside the once more of conduct, the advantages of a primarily based life-style, and provide sensible hints on how to come to be a grasp of your very non-public physical games. Welcome to the adventure of recurring living and to becoming a "Creature of Routine". Routines can range extensively from man or woman to individual, relying on their lifestyle, goals, and personal opportunities. Here are a few examples of physical video games:

1 Morning Routine: This need to encompass waking up at a selected time,

Doing some moderate stretching or workout, having a wholesome breakfast, and making plans the day in advance.

2 Work Routine: This might possibly include beginning the workday via checking emails, prioritizing duties for the day, taking normal breaks to maintain productivity, and wrapping

up the day with the aid of way of reviewing finished responsibilities and making equipped for day after today.

3 Exercise Routine: This can be a specific set of bodily sports completed at a sure time of day, a number of instances consistent with week. It might consist of a warmness-up, crucial exercising, and funky-down section.

four Evening Routine: This may want to comprise preparing and consuming dinner, spending time with own family or on interests, getting organized for the following day (like packing a lunch or choosing clothes), and a winding-down recurring earlier than bed, which encompass studying or meditation.

five Weekend Routine: This can also encompass chores, grocery shopping, meal prep for the upcoming week, social sports activities, and rest time.

Remember, the crucial aspect to an high-quality regular is consistency and ensuring it aligns collectively together with your dreams and lifestyle. It's additionally crucial to be bendy and regulate your regular as favored.

Creating a habitual that works for you entails understanding your private goals, manner of life, and options. Here are a few steps to help you create an powerful recurring:

1 Identify Your Goals: What do you want to benefit on the facet of your routine? It might be something from improving productiveness, retaining a healthy way of life, lowering stress, or simply bringing greater order in your day.

2 Understand Your Lifestyle: Consider your art work hours, own family commitments, and one-of-a-kind duties. Your normal should healthy seamlessly into your manner of lifestyles, not disrupt it.

three Start Small: If you're new to putting in workout routines, start with small, manageable duties. It's better to start with a few responsibilities that you can continuously entire than to create an prolonged list that feels overwhelming.

4 Consistency is Key: The strength of a regular comes from doing the equal subjects in the same order time and again once more. Consistency enables to assemble conduct

5 Be Flexible: Life is unpredictable, and your habitual ought to be flexible enough to deal with surprising adjustments. Don't be too tough on yourself in case you skip over a part of your ordinary. Just select up wherein you left off.

6 Review and Adjust: Regularly assessment you're regular to appearance if it's

Assisting you purchased your desires. Don't be afraid to make changes as wanted. Your routine has to evolve with you.

The purpose of a routine is to improve your life, not to restrict it. It wants to deliver you delight and delight, now not stress or tension.

Establishing a normal can take various quantities of time, counting on the individual and the complexity of the addiction being ordinary. According to a 2009 observe posted within the European Journal of Social Psychology, it takes anywhere from 18 to 254 days for someone to form a modern addiction. On commonplace, it takes approximately 66 days for a present day day conduct to grow to be automated.

However, it's critical to look at that those figures can range extensively. For instance, extremely good behavior may also take longer to shape, and some humans can be better perfect to forming behavior than others.

In terms of creating a everyday, many people locate it beneficial to plot out their recurring for as a minimum 3 weeks; this is usually how extended it takes in your routine to grow to be a everyday dependency for you.

As we stated in advance, the critical problem to putting in place a recurring is consistency and persistence. It's a way that requires time and effort, but the benefits may be large.

Staying endorsed at the same time as establishing a regular can every now and then be tough, but proper here are some recommendations that could assist:

1 Set Clear Goals: Having a easy information of why you're setting up a ordinary can offer motivation. Whether it's to decorate productivity, health, or not unusual nicely-being, preserves your goals in thoughts.

2 Start Small: Don't crush yourself with a complicated everyday right away. Start with small, capability duties and progressively upload more as you get cushty.

three Celebrate Small Wins: Every time you efficiently comply with your recurring, take a moment to famend your achievement. This can decorate your motivation and make the technique more a laugh.

four Be Flexible: Understand that it's okay if topics don't continually cross according to devise. Be inclined to regulate your regular as wanted.

five Visualize Success: Imagine the manner you'll revel in as soon as your regular is firmly set up. Visualization can be a powerful motivator.

6 Find a Routine Buddy: If feasible, discover someone who stocks your dreams. You can inspire every precise and preserve every exclusive responsible.

7 Don't Be Too Hard on Yourself: Remember, it's ordinary to have off days. Don't beat yourself up if you pass over an afternoon or. The essential element is to get again on course.

The key to putting in a ordinary is consistency. It is probably tough in the starting, however with time, it turns into 2d nature.

When on the lookout for to set up physical activities, people regularly make some common mistakes:

1 Setting Unrealistic Expectations: One of the most common mistakes is setting goals which may be too ambitious or unrealistic. It's essential to start small and regularly boom you're ordinary.

2 Lack of Consistency: Routines are all about consistency. Skipping your ordinary too frequently can prevent it from becoming a dependancy. Three Not Adapting the Routine: Life adjustments, and so must your regular. If some issue isn't operating, don't be afraid to alter your ordinary.

4 Ignoring Your Body Clock: Everyone has a natural rhythm, or body clock, which could have an effect on electricity degrees and productiveness. Ignoring this may make a habitual greater difficult to maintain.

5 Not Allowing for Flexibility: While consistency is high, it's also critical to permit for a few flexibility on your ordinary Life is unpredictable, and your routine must be able to accommodate that.

6 Neglecting Rest: It's crucial to include rest and relaxation in your everyday. Overworking can result in burnout and make it greater difficult to stick on your ordinary.

Let's say you've installed a morning recurring that includes a 30-minute exercise. However, you've currently started a present day task that requires you to start paintings in advance, making it tough to fit for your exercise.

Here's how you could regulate your everyday:

1 Evaluate Your Routine: Look at every a part of your normal and recollect its importance and versatility. In this situation, exercising is essential on your health, however it can possibly be moved to a remarkable time.

2 Consider Alternatives: Could you glide your exercising to the midnight, or ruin it up into smaller workout workouts at some point of the day? Maybe a quick 15-minute workout inside the morning and some specific 15

minutes after artwork should be simply right for you.

3 Test the New Routine: Try the adjusted ordinary for every week or and notice the way it works for you. Do you experience rushed within the morning, or are you able to control a while effectively?

4 Review and Adjust Again if Necessary: If the new ordinary isn't running, don't be afraid to make in addition modifications. Maybe you comprehend which you make a decision on an prolonged, single exercising consultation, so you determine to move your workout to the night time time after art work.

Keep in mind, the purpose of a recurring is to serve you and make your lifestyles much less complex, no longer to create more strain. It's ok to make modifications as desired until you find out what works exceptional for you.

Importance of Routines in Our Lives

Routines play a vital function in our lives, often serving because the backbone of productivity, overall performance, and nicely-being. Here's why they're so crucial:

Structure: Routines provide a experience of shape and order in our

Lives. By following a regular, we can put together our days round unique sports activities activities, which permits us manage our time extra efficiently.

Efficiency: Routines put off the want to devise and make picks approximately what task to carry out next, saving us valuable time and intellectual power. This improved overall performance can unfasten up time for rest, interests, or exclusive interests.

Habit Formation: Routines are the constructing blocks of conduct. By repeating the equal actions within the equal order, we're capable of form new conduct or alternate present ones. Habits, as soon as common, can characteristic mechanically, making it much less tough to preserve a desired behaviour.

Goal Achievement: Routines can help us gather our desires. Whether it's enhancing health, learning a brand new talent, or completing a venture, consistent workouts provide the field critical to make constant improvement and ultimately gain our goals.

Reduced Stress: Knowing what to anticipate and at the same time as to assume it could appreciably reduce pressure and tension Routines offer predictability, which could create a experience of manage and calm in a chaotic worldwide.

Health and Well-being: Regular workout routines round sleep, food plan, and exercise can drastically decorate physical fitness. Similarly, sporting events that embody mindfulness, relaxation, or pastimes can decorate highbrow fitness. In give up, workouts are greater than only a time table of sports. They are a device for reinforcing productiveness, fostering excessive top notch behavior, attaining dreams, lowering pressure, and selling not unusual fitness and well-being. Embracing the energy of exercise exercises can cause big improvements in both our personal and professional lives.

Let's delve deeper into the importance of exercises with a few examples:

1 Structure and Time Management: Consider a scholar who has a ordinary of studying for two hours every night time. This routine gives a easy form for the day and guarantees that point is ready aside for reading. It gets rid of the need for each day choice-making about even as to check, because of this saving time and highbrow strength.

2 Efficiency and Productivity: Imagine a creator who follows a strict ordinary of writing for 3 hours every morning while their thoughts is most up to date. This ordinary will growth performance through aligning the venture of writing with the writer's peak productivity hours. Over time, this may cause a great boom in output.

three Habit Formation and Behavior Change: Consider someone trying to lead a healthier manner of existence. They also can installation a ordinary of going for a run each morning and eating a healthy breakfast afterwards. Over time, the ones actions come to be normal, making it less hard to hold the contemporary, extra healthful behavior.

4 Goal Achievement: Think about a person who wants to research a brand new language. They can also create a routine of using a language-gaining knowledge of app for half-hour each day. This steady ordinary allows them make everyday improvement closer to their motive.

5 Reduced Stress and Improved Mental Health: A everyday of regular meditation or mindfulness can assist reduce strain and decorate highbrow health. For example, someone would probably installation a recurring of meditating for 20 mins each nighttime earlier than mattress to assist clean their mind and sell better sleep.

6 Physical Health and Well-being: Regular workout routines round sleep, eating regimen, and workout could have good sized fitness blessings. For instance, a habitual of getting 8 hours of sleep every night, consuming balanced meals, and workout for half of of-hour each day can boom energy levels, enhance temper, and reduce the danger of many health issues.

These examples illustrate how physical video games, whilst thoughtfully installed and constantly observed, can play a pivotal function in numerous aspects of our lives, from productivity and intention achievement to health and well being. They offer shape, sell accurate conduct, and might help us live more inexperienced, balanced, and desirable lives.

Overview of the Book

"The Creature of Routine: Mastering the Art of Habitual Living" is a complete guide that explores the profound effect of sporting activities on our lives. It delves into the technological know-how of conduct, the psychology of ordinary, and the artwork of efficaciously implementing them into our every day lives.

The ebook starts offevolved through defining what it way to be a "Creature of Routine", highlighting the importance of wearing sports in offering form, improving productiveness, and selling regular properly-being. It then provides practical advice on a way to create, preserve, and modify wearing events to wholesome person lifestyles and desires.

Chapter 7: The Science of Routine

How Routines Work in Our Brain

Routines are a sequence of moves that we carry out so regularly that they turn out to be almost automatic. This is possible due to the way our brains artwork at the same time as developing and processing exercises.

The Role of the Basal Ganglia

The basal ganglia, a group of systems in the thoughts, play a substantial feature within the formation of exercises. When we perform an motion, our thoughts sends signals via various pathways. The basal ganglia feature a sort of relay station, wherein those indicators are processed and the precise responses are sent out.

When we repeat an movement, the signal pathway inside the basal ganglia related to that motion turns into stronger. This is known as Hebb's rule: neurons that fireplace together, cord together. Over time, due to the fact the motion is repeated, the pathway will become so strong that the motion becomes automated - a everyday.

The Power of Dopamine

Dopamine, a neurotransmitter in the brain, moreover performs a important characteristic in dependancy formation. When we perform an movement that outcomes in a powerful final results, our mind releases dopamine.

This creates a feeling of satisfaction and praise.

The launch of dopamine not handiest makes us sense accurate, however it moreover strengthens the signal pathway inside the basal ganglia associated with the movement. This technique that moves that bring about a dopamine release are more likely to turn out to be carrying occasions.

The Habit Loop

The way of routine formation can be damaged down right right into a cycle referred to as the dependancy loop. The dependancy loop consists of 3 parts: the cue, the ordinary, and the praise.

1 The Cue: This is the reason that initiates the behavior. It is probably whatever from a selected time of day to a sure emotion. 2 The Routine: This is the behavior itself. It's the motion you take in reaction to the cue.

three The Reward: This is the great final results from the behavior. It's what your mind likes approximately the routine.

Understanding the dependancy loop is critical for getting to know the paintings of ordinary living. By identifying and manipulating the tremendous additives of the addiction loop, we will take control of our sports and, thru extension, our lives. Here are a few examples of appropriate conduct:

1 Exercising often can be as simple as doing ten to 15 pushups a day or following a established exercise regular.

2 Eating healthy consists of eating every day servings of end result and vegetables, getting ready nutritious and attractive food, and staying hydrated through way of eating enough water.

3 Practicing appropriate hygiene: This involves flossing your enamel at the least as soon as an afternoon, staying on top of grooming and bathing.

4 Getting adequate sleep: Ensuring you get at least 8 hours of sleep every night time time time.

5 Expressing gratitude: Telling your family which you appreciate them.

6 Practicing meditation: Daily meditation will will let you stay greater mindfully.

7 Reading books: If you want to pursue non-prevent boom.

8 Writing: If you want to grow to be a creator.

The key to forming precise behavior is to start small and grade by grade growth. It's moreover important to eliminate any boundaries that could prevent you from sticking for your habits. With staying power and consistency, the ones suitable behavior can reason significant changes to your lifestyles.

Remember that we mentioned earlier inside the e book, in keeping with a 2009 observe published within the European Journal of Social Psychology, it takes anywhere from 18 to 254 days for a person to form a ultra-modern-day dependancy.

The identical observe additionally concluded that, on commonplace, it takes 66 days for a state-of-the-art conduct to turn out to be automated. However, the time it takes can range considerably relying at the conduct, the man or woman, and the

conditions. For example, many individuals found it much less complicated to adopt the addiction of consuming a pitcher of water at breakfast than do 50 sit down down-u.S.A.After morning coffee. Some human beings are higher appropriate to forming behavior than others. So, it's critical to take into account that everybody's journey to forming a current-day addiction is unique.

Staying added on at the same time as trying to form a brand new dependancy may be tough, however right proper right here are a few techniques that would assist:

1 Set Realistic Intentions: Be realistic about what you could

reap. Some carrying occasions can grow to be behavior, however not all will. It takes staying power, strength of mind, and strength of mind.

2 Prepare for Roadblocks: Think approximately what has saved you from building this normal within the beyond. Work proactively to put off those boundaries before they show up.

three Support Your Efforts with Nudges: Use cues for your environment to remind you to do your new dependancy. Make the dependancy attractive, smooth, and exciting.

4 Never Miss a Habit Twice in a Row: This will maintain you on route.

5 Stick to a Sustainable Pace: That manner you acquired't burn out.

6 Think About Your Habit as a Way to Grow 1% Per Day: Improving handiest a touch bit each day consequences in big modifications over time.

7 Remember Why You Started: When you experience like quitting, consider why you started out.

eight Have Fun!: Do a few thing you like.

nine Search for Inspiration:

Notice others who have made changes and be inspired thru way of their difficult artwork and dedication.

Here are a few sensible techniques for growing and maintaining healthy wearing activities:

1 Start Small: Changing your routine all of sudden might not yield lasting

outcomes. Instead, choose one small element each week to paintings on. It might be which encompass a few component new and extraordinary, or slicing out a awful dependancy.

2 Add to Existing Habits: You likely have already got some behavior worked into your ordinary. Try adding new behavior to offer ones. For example, if you need to check extra, you may set apart ten mins to have a look at at the equal time as you have got your coffee.

3 Make Swaps: Think approximately the property you do within the route of the day that aren't so healthful and transfer them with higher behaviors. For example, if you enjoy gradual inside the afternoons and

consume sugary snacks for a fast select-me-up, strive taking a brisk walk as an alternative.

4 Plan Ahead: When existence receives traumatic, you may be tempted to skip out on the trendy additives of your each day routine. By doing things like prepping meals earlier of time, deciding on out an outfit the night time earlier than artwork, or having an exchange home workout choice for the instances you can't make it to the gym, you help set yourself up for achievement.

five Make Time for Things You Enjoy: Even if it's just 15 minutes a day, set apart time to do something you locate a laugh or enjoyable. This will launch chemical messengers on your frame which can be pinnacle for your bodily and intellectual health.

6 Reward Yourself for Small Victories: Set dreams and feature a extraordinary time on the identical time as you achieve them. Have you added exercise for your weekly normal and worked out each day as deliberate for the closing couple weeks? Treat yourself!

7 Don't Beat Yourself Up If You Miss a Day: Making life modifications may be hard and you might forget about to do a little issue this is new on your ordinary each once in a while. Remember, the vital component to forming correct behavior is consistency.

eight Find Out Why Your New Habits Haven't Stuck So Far: Before you start a present day ordinary, you want to consider why you had been not able to paste to a new ordinary in the beyond. Once you address those problems, everything will deal with itself.

9 Give Your Routine a Purpose: When you recognize the advantages of a healthful regular for your intellectual and bodily health and how it assist you to gain your desires, you'll be more devoted to preserving your guarantees to yourself.

10 Go Slow but Steady : Look at the belongings you're already doing right and assemble on them. A new recurring doesn't should contain in reality new subjects.

There are numerous commonplace boundaries that humans often encounter while trying to form a state-of-the-art dependancy:

1 Perfectionism: Many people fall into the entice of all-or-not some thing

questioning. They recollect that if they might't do some thing perfectly, they shouldn't do it the least bit. This can bring about procrastination and avoidance of the ultra-cutting-edge habit.

2 Lack of Knowledge: Not understanding the manner to deal with horrific feelings can be a large barrier to addiction formation. It's crucial to discover ways to gadget those emotions in location of heading off them.

three Negativity Bias: This is a bent to attention extra on horrible research than excellent ones. It need to make it hard to peer improvement and hold motivation.

four External Barriers: These can include time constraints, monetary costs, weather conditions, loss of area, and physical pain. It's crucial to count on the ones boundaries and function a plan to deal with them.

5 Lack of Self-Compassion: It's regular to revel in u.S.A.And downs at the equal time as trying to form a brand new habit. Being tough on your self at a few level in the down instances can keep away from your development. Remember to be patient and compassionate with your self.

6 Lack of Self-Discipline and Commitment: Forming a brand new habit requires persistence, strength of thoughts, and resolution. It's crucial to prepare for roadblocks and art work proactively to take away the ones limitations earlier than they display up.

To overcome the ones boundaries, it could be beneficial to set practical intentions, start with smaller micro-conduct, block time on your calendar to workout the conduct, and be compassionate with yourself.

Remember, forming a cutting-edge-day dependancy is a journey, now not a holiday spot. Be affected character with yourself and feature fun your progress along the way.

Tracking your development in forming a new dependancy can be a effective motivator and a terrific manner to preserve yourself accountable. Here are a few methods you can use:

1 Habit Tracker: A addiction tracker is a easy manner to degree whether or not or not you probable did a dependancy. The most fundamental layout is to get a calendar and bypass off every day you stay along with your normal. For example, if you meditate on Monday, Wednesday, and Friday, every of those dates gets an X. As time rolls through, the calendar turns into a document of your addiction streak.

2 Journaling: Consider using a magazine to song your wholesome behavior and productivity desires. Seeing your progress can

give you a feel of feat and assist you stay inspired.

3 Apps: There are many apps to be had that let you track your conduct. These apps regularly include skills like reminders, streaks, and seen representations of your progress.

4 Visual Reminders: Hang up your dependancy tracker someplace you'll see it every day, and then begin tracking your development. Use a check mark or a fun decal to mark every day that you complete your each day addiction. Once you begin racking up a sequence of consecutive days, you acquired't want to break it!

Remember, the key to forming specific behavior is consistency. So, locate a method that works splendid for you and live with it.

Let's say you're trying to shape a dependancy of reading for half of of-hour each day. You've been a hit for in step with week, and your dependancy tracker is beginning to show a pleasing chain of consecutive days. But then, subsequently, you've got a busy time table, and it appears no longer viable to discover half of-hour to have a look at.

Here's how you may maintain the chain going:

1 Adjust Your Goal: Instead of aiming for half-hour, reason to have a have a look at for truely 5 mins. The important trouble isn't always to pass the addiction sincerely. 2 Find Idle Time: Use idle time to your benefit. Maybe you could test at the same time as commuting or expecting an appointment. Three Prioritize: Make your addiction a problem. If reading is essential to you, you will probable need to sacrifice some factor else in your time table.

4 Use Reminders: Set a reminder for your phone or write a look at to your self. This can help ensure you don't forget about to complete your addiction.

The aim isn't always to be best, but to be ordinary. Even if you may't do as an awful lot as you'd like, performing some bit can despite the fact that help hold your addiction and keep your chain going.

For individuals who are focused on their health, adopting healthful conduct can deliver numerous rewards, along with:

1 Heart Health: Following a wholesome healthy eating plan can assist shield the heart doubtlessly preventing up to 80% of untimely coronary heart sickness and stroke diagnoses.

2 Reduced Risk of Diseases: Healthy behavior can also guard you from intense health troubles like weight troubles and diabetes. They can also reduce the risk of pleasant illnesses.

3 Better Mood: A healthful diet plan can growth your mood. Engaging in powerful self-speak even as you enjoy insecure, disturbing, or afraid about a few element can also be a beneficial highbrow dependancy.

4 Improved Physical Appearance: Healthy conduct can improve your physical appearance.

5 Increased Energy Levels: New conduct, like healthy consuming and everyday bodily interest, also allow you to control your weight and function greater strength.

6 Improved Mental Wellness: Some behavior can promote physical and highbrow well being.

7 Longevity: Certain preventative conduct also can promote an extended lifestyles by using manner of the usage of assisting push back undesirable health problems.

8 Improved Productivity: Some conduct may additionally help you better control a while and obtain your dreams.

Remember, the secret is consistency. It might probable take the time to look the consequences; however the rewards are properly nicely absolutely well worth the try!

Chapter 8: The Power of Routine

In our day by day lives, we often underestimate the electricity of workouts. They are the invisible form of our lives, imparting a solid framework that shapes our movements and behaviors. This bankruptcy will discover how sporting sports can significantly have an effect on our behavior, the use of real-lifestyles examples of success humans who've harnessed the energy of sporting occasions.

So, just like infants, adults also can extensively gain from having a normal. It gives form, reduces pressure, and might bring about more healthy and happier lives. The energy of habitual isn't always simply beneficial for toddlers, however for adults as properly. Here are some reasons why:

1. Efficiency: When we've a everyday that we comply with every day, it

Reduces the need to make decisions each day It permits us to recognize exactly what obligations we want to do each day on the same time as no longer having to contemplate, decide or think an excessive amount of.

2. Reduces Need to Plan: A set habitual gets rid of the want to plot our sports each morning and fee range and allocate our valuable time.

three. Creates Structure: A every day recurring offers structure and a logical series in our lives. It offers the framework within which we live our lives and conduct our each day sports.

4. Saves Time: Time is the maximum treasured asset at our disposal. By following a regular, we free up time that could in any other case be spent on planning, preference-making and education.

5. Instills Good Habits: The thriller to constructing true behavior is repetition. When we layout a personal everyday that works for us, it allows growing well habits with the useful useful resource of

encouraging us to replicate the equal obligations again and again once more.

6. Reduces Stress: If you have a plan, you'll enjoy more on pinnacle of things. You might also have made many choices earlier, and you can focus on making nicely options for those that live.

7. Improves Sleep: Keeping a normal sleep schedule is step one toward being better rested.

eight. Promotes Health: Meal making plans makes it less difficult to paste to a healthful weight loss plan, however which means that that putting aside time for buying and meal prep.

9. Boosts Happiness: If you have got have been given a time table, you may build in time for play. Downtime is good in your highbrow health.

The Influence of Routines on Behavior

Routines are powerful gear that could have an effect on our conduct. They provide shape and a experience of predictability, reducing the quantity of choices we want to make every day. This can unfasten up highbrow strength for additional essential responsibilities. For instance, keep in mind the routine of brushing your teeth every morning and night. This smooth addiction, over time, influences your behavior thru instilling a sense of discipline and promoting dental fitness. Routines can absolutely play a important feature in promoting health. Consistent physical activities spherical mealtimes and workout could make it less complicated to keep a wholesome manner of lifestyles. For example, a ordinary sleep regular contributes to a greater healthy sleep cycle, this is important for bodily health and intellectual nicely-being.

Routines are just like the invisible form of each day life, providing a shape that can be distinctly useful. They streamline our recognition, guiding us through the day and decreasing the want to plot every unmarried element. This efficiency leaves us with extra intellectual strength for particular duties, improving our productivity.

Moreover, sporting activities instill proper conduct. The thriller to constructing those behavior lies inside the repetition that sports necessitate. Over time, these repeated behaviors grow to be 2d nature,

One of the maximum vast influences of exercising workouts is their capacity to lessen pressure. When we've were given a plan, we experience extra in control. We've made many alternatives earlier, allowing us to popularity on the present 2nd and the choices that stay. This enjoy of control can appreciably lessen feelings of strain and tension.

Furthermore, workouts can improve happiness. By scheduling time for relaxation and leisure sports, we make sure that we're searching after our intellectual health. This downtime can beautify our common happiness and life delight.

In the area of conduct control, in particular for children, workouts are a godsend. They offer a revel in of safety and help children apprehend what's anticipated of them, making conduct management less tough for dad and mom and caregivers.

Lastly, exercises decorate our capability to pursue and gather our dreams. They provide a roadmap to follow, making the adventure in the direction of our goals seem extra possible. Each finished routine looks like a small victory, bringing us one step inside the direction of our targets.

In end, the strength of exercise routines extends an extended way past clean time control. They shape our movements, impact our behaviors, and ultimately, play a huge function in identifying our fulfillment and happiness.

day into factors, dedicating half of of to SpaceX and half to Tesla.

These examples display that a achievement people from numerous fields have harnessed the power of sports to enhance their productiveness and fulfillment. They recognize the importance of consistency, vicinity, and the effective use of time.

The advantages of being a creature of habitual

Being a creature of routine has severa benefits. It reduces choice fatigue, as having a recurring manner you have got got fewer selections to make every day. This leaves extra highbrow strength for crucial obligations. Routines moreover provide a experience of manipulate and predictability in an unpredictable worldwide, decreasing strain and tension.

Moreover, workouts can assist us attain our desires. Whether it's a health motive, a profession goal, or a non-public improvement purpose, having a recurring that facilitates that motive can appreciably increase our opportunities of success. For example, in case you need to grow to be extra healthful, having a ordinary that includes ordinary workout and healthy eating allow you to obtain that aim.

In cease, being a creature of ordinary is not about being inflexible or rigid. It's about know-how the energy of conduct and using them to our gain. It's about developing a life that shows our values and aspirations. So, permit's encompassing the power of ordinary and come to be masters of recurring dwelling.

Being a creature of habitual should have numerous advantages in severa additives of lifestyles, together with work, college, and domestic:

At Work:

1. Increased Productivity: A routine can help you set up priorities, restrict procrastination, and maintain song of your goals.

2. Time Management: By having a hard and fast time table for obligations, you can control a while extra effectively.

3. Reduced Need for Planning: When high quality duties turn out to be recurring, you spend much less time making plans and extra time doing.

At School:

1. Better Learning: Having a check everyday can cause more powerful getting to know and progressed academic normal performance.

2. Reduced Stress: Knowing what to expect and at the same time as can help lessen strain and tension round schoolwork.

3. Improved Focus: A routine can assist student's consciousness on responsibilities handy in location of worrying approximately what's subsequent.

At Home:

1. Work-Life Balance: A everyday can assist ensure you have time for all of the critical

matters in your lifestyles, including relaxation and personal hobbies.

2. Healthier Habits: Regular mealtimes and exercise schedules can result in more healthy behavior.

3. Better Sleep: Going to bed and waking up at the same time each day can enhance the exceptional of your sleep.

Here are some tips on a manner to set up workouts at paintings, college, and domestic:

At Work:

Understand Your Energy Levels: Pay interest to the way you revel in for the duration of the day and suit obligations together with your temper and stage of motivation.

Make Mornings Effortless: Establish a morning recurring that allows you start your day at the equal time as not having to make many small picks.

Set Priorities for the Day: Identify the top three maximum crucial

At School:

1. Establish Clear Expectations: Make fantastic university students understand what's predicted of them within the study room.

2. Create a Predictable Environment: Routines offer a set up environment, permitting university students to revel in strong and regular. Three. Enhance Efficiency: Clear techniques preserve precious academic time and decrease disruptions.

4. Foster Independence: Students discover ways to navigate classroom duties independently through way of putting in location regular look at room sports.

5. Identify Critical Areas: Reflect on the particular areas wherein physical activities and techniques are wished, which includes morning get right of entry to, transitions, materials manipulate, institution art work, and have a look at room discussions.

At Home:

1. Identify Important Daily Activities: Figure out what you need to get finished every day, every at domestic and at artwork, and while.

2. Structure Your Day: Group your responsibilities into the time of day that makes the maximum sense for at the same time as you could efficiently whole them.

1. Get Specific: Get as particular as you want together together with your define of responsibilities. For example, write a every day morning ordinary that appears a few detail like this to account for time: 6:00: Wake up, bathe 6:30: Breakfast, brush enamel 7:00: Leave the residence.

2. Plan Out Your Routine on a Longer Time-Scale: Decide what desires to be executed each day, weekly, biweekly, month-to-month, every year, and so forth And agenda this all out.

3. Incorporate Healthy Habits: Fitting in a workout which consist of yoga, cycling, or ground bodily video video games like lunges

Making a healthful breakfast like eggs or greens. Journaling to lessen pressure or exercising affirmations.

Remember, the reason of a ordinary isn't to agenda each second of your day, but as an alternative to discover a balance that allows for flexibility when desired. It's approximately developing a shape that works for you and permits you stay your high-quality life.

Routines could have a giant impact on severa styles of relationships:

Romantic Relationships:

Routines can offer balance and familiarity, which can be key substances in maintaining an extended-time period devoted dating.

Sharing experiences and tasty in sports activities on the side of your companion create a sense of togetherness and consequences in stepped forward intimacy.

Routines moreover assist create a revel in of consistency and reliability in the dating, primary to more keep in mind.

Family Relationships:

Family sporting activities can assist youngsters experience more secure due to the reality they apprehend what to anticipate.

Certain research have associated own family exercises with parenting competence and marital pleasure.

Friendships:

Regular meetups or sports activities can beautify bonds and make certain that you hold in touch. It also can reason shared recollections and opinions, deepening the friendship.

Professional Relationships:

In a work putting, workout workouts can assist installation easy expectancies and enhance performance, leading to better teamwork and collaboration.

However, it's crucial to endure in mind that not all carrying activities are created identical, and failing to have a have a look at or regulate our behavior could have a limiting effect on our lives. It's about finding the right stability and being open to change on the same time as vital.

Here are a few more tips on a way to installation exercises and stay with them:

1. Set Realistic Goals: Before you begin developing your routine, choose out

what you need to accumulate. Your desires can also want to variety from becoming more powerful, getting into form, or dwelling a greater suit existence.

2. Write Down Your Daily Activities: If you have already got obligations you need to do every day or if there are belongings you need to start doing each day, jot the ones down in a listing and use it to devise out your ordinary.

three. Create a Daily To-Do List: Many people locate it beneficial to write down down the each day tasks they set out for themselves; this will feature a normal reminder of your recurring and furthermore give you the satisfaction of being capable of flow into completed gadgets off the listing.

4. Start Small: Begin with one week at a time and start small – that way you may construct on easy accomplishments.

5. Be Consistent with Time: If you need to get a each day stroll in, try it at the identical time each day.

6. Prepare for Roadblocks: Think about what has stored you from building this routine in the past. Work proactively to dispose of the ones barriers earlier than they display up.

Chapter 9: Becoming a Creature of Routine

Step-via-step manual at the manner to set up exercises 1. Identify Your Goals: The first step in setting up a ordinary is to pick out what you want to advantage. This can be something from enhancing your fitness, to studying a ultra-cutting-edge capability, or engaging in a chunk-related cause. This is a huge goal and could manual the creation of your routine.

2. Break Down Your Goals into Tasks: discover your dreams,

Smash them down into smaller achievable duties.

These duties will form the basis of your recurring.

Now, you need to interrupt down your extensive purpose into

Smaller, actionable responsibilities For example, if you have a fitness aim, the ones obligations ought to embody exercising for 1/2-hour every day, devour a healthful food regimen, get eight hours of sleep every night time time time

3. Prioritize Your Tasks: Not all obligations are created same. Some are extra vital than others in supporting you bought your dreams. Prioritize your obligations primarily based mostly on their importance and urgency. In our fitness example, all obligations are important,

However you may likely prioritize exercise because it's the location wherein you could need the maximum improvement.

4. Schedule Your Tasks: Now which you have your obligations and their

Priorities, it's time to time table them into your day.

Try to time table your most crucial duties for whilst you are maximum efficient. This consists of identifying whilst you'll do each venture. You can also decide to workout inside the morning because of the reality that's when you have the most power, eat healthful meals during the day, and make certain you're in mattress early sufficient to get eight hours of sleep.

5. Stick to Your Schedule: Consistency is crucial as regards to installing physical games. Try to paste for your agenda as a extraordinary deal as feasible. Remember, it's ok in case you leave out an afternoon or . The important issue is to get once more on route as soon as you could. This is frequently the hardest detail. It calls for location and consistency.

Tips on a manner to stick with exercise routines

1. Start Small: Don't attempt to overhaul your complete life suddenly. Start with small adjustments and step by step boom to massive ones. If your goal is to begin a each day exercising ordinary, don't start with the aid of way of trying to workout consultation for an hour every single day. Instead, start with some component small and capacity, like 10 minutes of exercise an afternoon. Once

you've installed that dependancy, you could regularly growth the period of your wearing activities.

2. Be Consistent: Consistency is vital close to sticking to workouts. Try to do your duties at the equal time every day to help them turn out to be a dependancy.

Consistency is essential in forming a brand new dependancy. If you're seeking to set up a routine of reading earlier than bed, try to do it at the identical time every night time time time time. This is probably, as an example, constantly beginning your reading at nine:30 PM. Over time, this can grow to be a addiction and also you'll find yourself surely gravitating toward a e book at that time.

three. Reward Yourself: Give yourself praise at the same time as you preserve on together with your regular. This is probably something from a address, to a few day off, or maybe simplest a pat at the all over again.

Rewards may be a remarkable motivator. If you've stuck for your routine of ingesting healthy for a whole week, praise yourself with a deal with over the weekend. This doesn't propose you need to take pleasure in unhealthy meals, but possibly you could have that piece of dark chocolate you've been yearning. The idea is to partner sticking on your normal with excellent reinforcement.

4. Be Flexible: Life is unpredictable and now and again subjects don't pass according to plot. Be flexible and inclined to modify your ordinary as desired.

Life is unpredictable and there are probably instances at the same time as your normal receives disrupted. For instance, if you generally pass for a run outside but it's raining closely in the future, be bendy and do an indoor workout as an alternative. The key is not to allow minor disruptions derail your complete routine.

Dealing with boundaries and disruptions to sports activities

1. Anticipate Obstacles: Think approximately what might in all likelihood disrupt your ordinary and function a plan for a way to address it.

If you're seeking to set up a habitual of going for a morning run, capability limitations should encompass terrible weather or feeling ill. To cope with the ones, you could have a backup plan like having exercising movement pics ready to do at home if you can't run outside, or permitting yourself to take damage if you're not feeling nicely but developing a dedication to start once more as speedy as you're better.

2. Be Resilient: If your routine receives disrupted, don't surrender. Get decrease again on tr ack as quickly as you could.

Disruptions are a part of life and it's essential to no longer allow them to completely derail your development. For example, in case you're in search of to keep a wholesome consuming ordinary but you have an afternoon in that you take pride in junk meals, don't recall the entire ordinary a failure. Instead, make strength of will to get again on direction collectively together with your next meal.

3. Seek Support: If you're locating it hard to stick to your recurring, don't be afraid to be looking for help. This can be from a friend, family member, or expert

Reaching out to others can be very beneficial. For example, in case you're in search of to establish a look at recurring, you can shape a have a look at enterprise with buddies. This now not fine makes the undertaking extra fun however moreover creates a enjoy of duty.

Remember, turning into a creature of ordinary is a adventure, not a holiday spot. It's about making small, ordinary modifications that add up through the years. So be affected character with yourself and feature a laugh your improvement alongside the way.

Chapter 10: Beyond Routine

The Importance of Flexibility and Adaptability internal Routines

While workouts offer shape and assist us gain our dreams, it's in addition essential to be flexible and adaptable. Life is unpredictable and there are probably instances whilst sticking for your ordinary won't be possible. For instance, if you have a ordinary of going for a morning run however wake up in the destiny to a heavy downpour, it's vital to evolve and maybe transfer to an indoor exercise rather.

Another instance might be a normal of cooking healthful food at home. If at some point you find out yourself walking late and now not able to cook dinner, in place of resorting to risky rapid meals, you may adapt through having a few healthy, easy-to-put together meals accessible for such conditions.

Flexibility and flexibility internal sports are essential for numerous motives:

1. Life is Unpredictable: Despite our fine efforts, existence often throws

Curveballs our way. An surprising art work venture, a own family emergency, or maybe some element as smooth as horrific weather can disrupt our sporting events. In such situations, being bendy permits us to conform our workout routines in desire to leaving in the back of them without a doubt. For example, in case you generally go to the health club inside the middle of the night, but must artwork past due ultimately, you may awaken early the subsequent morning to make up for the left out workout.

2. Prevents Burnout: Sticking rigidly to a routine, mainly a

Worrying one, can result in burnout over time. Flexibility allows us to provide ourselves a damage while needed. For instance, if you've been analyzing intensively for exams, it's essential to provide yourself a time without work to loosen up and recharge.

three. Caters to Changing Goals and Priorities: Our goals and priorities can alternate over the years What appeared crucial a few months in the past won't maintain the identical importance now. Being adaptable permits us to regulate our workouts to align with the ones converting desires. For instance, in case your initial aim modified into weight reduction however you're now greater interested in constructing energy, you will want to comply your exercise and weight loss plan normal consequently.

4. Allows for Personal Growth: Sometimes, stepping out of our habitual can bring about new tales and private increase. This may be as easy as attempting out a current interest in choice to searching TV within the night time. These new stories can upload fee to our lives or even decorate our bodily games.

In essence, even as sporting activities provide a enjoy of form and manage, it's essential to balance them with flexibility and versatility to navigate the unpredictability of lifestyles efficiently.

This balance guarantees that our sporting events serve us and now not the alternative way round.

Balancing Routine and Spontaneity

While routines are beneficial, it's additionally important to go away room for spontaneity in existence. Spontaneity lets in for creativity, fun, and the delight of sudden critiques.

For example, you may in all likelihood have a weekend ordinary of cleaning and grocery shopping. But if a chum invitations you for a spontaneous road revel in, it can be an top notch concept to head for it. You can commonly capture up on your chores later.

Similarly, when you have a strict artwork regular, taking an impromptu time off to spend with circle of relatives or to pursue a interest can offer a far-desired spoil and can really growth your productivity in the end.

In quit, on the identical time as turning into a creature of recurring has its advantages, it's critical to undergo in thoughts that bodily video games serve us, now not the other manner round Being flexible, adaptable, and thinking of spontaneity guarantees that we don't in reality stay a disciplined existence, however also a satisfying one. Balancing routine and spontaneity is all about developing a harmonious aggregate of structure and freedom for your lifestyles. Here's why it's essential and the way you can acquire it:

1. Prevents Monotony: While exercise exercises provide form, sticking to

the identical everyday day in and day experience can become monotonous through the years. Spontaneity presents an element of wonder and pleasure to lifestyles. For instance, when you have a recurring of cooking at home every day, attempting a new restaurant spontaneously can destroy the monotony and make your routine extra exciting.

2. Boosts Creativity: Spontaneity often consequences in creativity. Breaking a ways from your recurring to attempt something new can reason sparkling thoughts and perspectives. For instance, in case you're a author with a strict writing every day, taking a spontaneous time off to visit a museum or artwork gallery need to offer new thought for your art work.

3. Enhances Flexibility: Incorporating spontaneity for your lifestyles must make you extra adaptable to exchange. For instance, when you have a strict exercise normal however inside the future your gymnasium is closed, being open

to trying a modern day exercise magnificence or going for a run out of doors can keep your health desires on direction.

four. Promotes Balance: Life isn't quite a whole lot productivity and engaging in goals.

It's additionally approximately enjoying the adventure. Balancing habitual and spontaneity guarantees you're now not just residing to paintings, but also walking to live. For instance, whilst it's vital to have a ordinary for paintings or observe, it's further critical to have spontaneous moments of relaxation and fun.

Remember, the key's stability. Too an lousy lot ordinary can result in burnout, while too much spontaneity can bring about chaos. Finding the proper balance amongst routine and spontaneity can reason a satisfying and green existence.

Incorporating spontaneity into your ordinary doesn't mean you want to make drastic changes. Here are some strategies you could upload a dash of spontaneity for your every day ordinary:

1. Try Something New: This might be as easy as trying a brand new food,

Analyzing a ebook out of doors of your normal genre, or taking a high-quality

1. Route to work. These small modifications can carry a experience of novelty and satisfaction on your day.

2. Be Open to Opportunities: If an unexpected possibility comes your way, be open to it. This will be an impromptu lunch with a pal, a final-minute journey, or a unexpected risk to analyze some component new.

3. Schedule Free Time: This could probable sound counterintuitive even as talking about carrying occasions but scheduling some 'loose time' can give you the freedom to be spontaneous. During this time, you could do anything you sense like without any plans or rules.

four. Break Your Routine Occasionally: While exercises are useful, it's ok to break them on occasion. If you usually spend your weekends cleansing and organizing, take a spontaneous break day to lighten up and perform a little component fun.

5. Practice Mindfulness: Being present inside the 2nd also can bring about spontaneity. Instead of constantly considering what's next to your time table, take some time to experience the existing 2d This need to motive spontaneous choices that supply pride and exhilaration.

Chapter 11: A New Day to Stay

When people keep in mind every day, they believe a few details uninteresting and stupid, but it really is wherein they will be wrong. When you find out a manner to apply triggers and keys efficiently, you may examine the real method for achievement.

Our mind is a real gadget. When you go to a store and purchase any gadget, unwrap it and take it out of the field, you will see that it comes with a person manual; this way, you could installation and use it yourself without the need for a technician. However, you got right here into the world with the maximum modern-day device in the Universe and also you slightly apprehend a way to apply it, or worse, you use it in the worst possible manner; it's like having a Ferrari and no longer understanding the manner to force. Well, our thoughts dreams preliminary instructions to automate strategies.

When we are more youthful, we're encouraged to learn. Our mother and father say: "Get accurate grades, be devoted, obedient and success is confident"; When we input college, the teachers say: "Be right, memorize my content cloth and get particular grades, and success might be assured", and the majority researches this manner, then the large hassle takes location, because success is not sufficient. Most CDFs are not a hit in simple phrases and clearly due to the fact amount of content material cloth is not like software functionality, or instead, "strength of action", but the worst of all is that each one the information and thoughts surpassed on thru humans of authority from our early life have end up computerized in our thoughts. Maybe you do no longer know it, but this notable effective gadget called the mind, in an incredible advent began out to automate techniques so you do now not need to waste energy. I'll provide you with an example: each day earlier than going to sleep you visit the rest room, take out your super toothbrush and brush your tooth, all with out questioning. The most fantastic thing of all is that, if you are used to brushing your tooth 37 times, on every occasion you could get very close to that variety, amongst 35 and 39 instances (the famous percentage factors plus or minus), so you can see the execution ability of the mind.

And we grow up on this intellectual version, acquiring horrible behavior, repeating everything, day by day, be it ingesting sugary meals, mendacity at the sofa after artwork, yelling at our youngsters... A majority of those conduct shape your recurring and on a day by day basis you bypass killing yourself a piece at a time. Here in this ebook you may take a look at the following technique: When we are greater youthful, we are counseled to study. Our parents say: "Get actual grades, be committed, obedient and fulfillment is assured"; When we enter college, the lecturers say: "Be correct, memorize my content material and get properly grades, and success can be guaranteed", and the majority studies this manner, then the big problem takes place, due to the reality fulfillment is not sufficient. Most CDFs aren't a achievement in smooth terms and in reality due to the truth amount of content isn't much like utility capability, or instead, "energy of motion", however the worst of all is that each one the facts and ideas passed on thru humans of authority from our formative years have come to be automated in our thoughts. Maybe you do now not recognize it, but this terrific effective tool called the brain, in an outstanding introduction began out out to automate strategies so you do not want to waste energy. I'll come up with an example: each day before going to sleep you go to the toilet, take out your incredible toothbrush and brush your enamel, all without thinking. The most terrific trouble of all is that, in case you are used to brushing your teeth 37 times, whenever you could get very close to that quantity, between 35 and 39 times (the famous percentage elements plus or minus), so that you can see the execution capability of the thoughts.

And we broaden up in this highbrow version, obtaining   horrible   behavior,   repeating everything, on a every day foundation, be it ingesting sugary food, lying on the couch after art work, yelling at our children... Most of those behavior shape your ordinary and each day you circulate killing your self a hint at a time. Here in this ebook you can research the following technique:

"It isn't possible for a man to look at what he thinks he already is aware of." (Epictetus)

A girl as soon as moved to a cave within the mountains to research from a guru. She informed him she preferred to examine the whole lot there has been to recognize. The guru passed her stacks of books and left her on my own so she need to take a look at. Every morning, he went to the cave to inspect the girl's development. He carried a heavy stick in his hand. Every morning I requested her the identical query:

Have you located out the whole lot but?

Every morning, her reaction turn out to be the equal:

No not yet.

The guru then hit her head with the stick.

This repeated for months. One day, the guru entered the cave, requested the identical query, heard the identical answer and raised the stick with hit inside the identical way, however the lady grabbed it earlier than it touched her head.

Relieved to keep away from the day's beating, however scared of reprisal, the lady checked out the guru. To his marvel, the guru changed into smiling.

"Congratulations," he stated. You graduated. Now everything you need to apprehend.

Like this? requested the lady.

You located out that you will never observe the entirety there's to recognize he spoke back. And he determined out the manner to prevent his pain.

This parable takes us lower lower back to a clean state of affairs, one of the most magnificent triggers of people: they may be pushed by using clean subjects, heading off pain and having pride. If you are now maintaining this ebook it's far due to the truth you are searching out a method to three pain you're presently experiencing or looking for to improve your records to have greater satisfaction; It's instinctive, it's miles from our reptilian mind.

The funniest detail of all is that everyone is brilliant at giving recommendation, guiding people, all of us is aware about exactly what's preventing their route and the way to get round it, however few do what desires to be finished, they stay stuck in their little bubble, as even though the complete global had to come to their door and produce them answers. However, this is not the manner it happens, I see and characteristic seen many individuals who need topics, but, of those human beings, only a few pay the actual price to have what they want. You can obtain as actual with one element: incredible topics take strive, approach, recognition, preliminary area and a incredible cause to be accomplished and, in case you are not willing to try this, you can furthermore not be able to taste the candy end result of this victory.

You may be questioning what "preliminary area" is. So I'm going to inform you a touch story and perhaps you may find out masses with it.

A little records earlier than the story as a way to mirror on: in step with IBGE, among 2003 and 2019, the percentage of obese human beings within the united states of america's populace aged 20 or over more than doubled, going from 12.2% to 26.Eight%. During the length, girl obesity extended from 14.Five% to 30.2% and remained above male weight problems, which rose from nine.6% to 22.Eight%.

The percentage of overweight humans within the populace aged 20 or over rose from 40 3.3% to sixty one.7% within the equal 17 years. Among men, it went from forty three.Three% to 60% and, amongst women, from 40 3.2% to sixty three.3%.

One Saturday morning, I were given up very early, absolutely out of my ordinary (which became napping past due and resting from the boring art work week), I left the residence, appeared up, the sky modified into blue, there were few clouds and the sun it glowed splendidly. Okay, I jumped proper away, like a Phoenix, saying to myself, in reality ecstatic: in recent times the whole thing modifications, I'm going to emerge as an athlete, examine 30 books a month, make an additional income, no person can save you me!

I speedy another time to my room, positioned on my fitness center garments (which with the useful resource of the manner have been quite dusty), then went to the rest room, washed my face, devoured my espresso and went out into the street. I positioned it in my mind: in recent times I'm going to walk 5 kilometers, no, I belief I'm going to run, due to the fact I'm superb! Damn, I couldn't final a hundred meters. Heart leaping out of my chest, heavy breathing and 1/2 a dozen swear words sum up my first race. A tragedy! Well, I saved strolling and reflecting on how I allowed myself to get to that kingdom. I returned from this experience sad and satisfied at the identical time satisfied that I had succeeded and sad about my overall performance, however I ought to admit that my athletic spark amazing lasted that day. The following few days I spent in ache and strolling like a lame duck.

That wasn't the simplest experience I had about it. I once got it into my head that I emerge as going to start operating out. I went to a gym, checked out the to be had plans and informed the secretary that I favored to pay for three months in advance, as long as they gave me a discount. She seemed me up and down, that brief evaluation, and have to have notion: "That obese man received't ultimate weeks, I'll supply him a discount!" Well, I paid proper there, I had blood in my eyes. And behold, once more my determination lasted subsequently, then in no manner again.

Today, subjects have changed, I visit the fitness center often, but I normally see humans there who start determinedly on Monday and, even as it's Wednesday, they now not move. This is so not unusual to appearance, I understand what goes via their heads. In an antique gym that I used to teach at, I become talking about people's thoughts, because of the truth I located that usually within the months of October, November and the forestall of January, people visit the gym en masse; When they get there, they inform the teacher that they need their frame like this, like this, until summer season or until Carnival. I nevertheless undergo in thoughts to at the existing time what the teacher replied to them: "Look, we're going to work, but only God does miracles...". He became right, first-rate God can do miracles, there can be no way to attain such brief effects with out a properly-defined technique, especially if you've in no manner had the dependancy of exercise.

Dear reader, you can see that I ended up going in opposition to the grain of maximum humans: even as the IBGE facts elements to a weight advantage, I lost 100 and twenty pounds and feature in truth reached eighty kilos, with out cheating, with out use of any type. Of substance, only the initial trouble, automation and consistent execution.

Our thoughts desires to research, if you do now not offer the proper instructions, the script, it does no longer look at, no man or woman can hold location one hundred% of the time, you want to discover ways to leave computerized to your thoughts what empowers you, so you will accumulate each ever more excellence. But, to make some thing automated, an initial attempt is vital till this technique will become included into your highbrow system; From then on, the try to perform the hobby becomes heaps much less and plenty lots less and automatic.

I like to use the plane metaphor: even as the plane takes to the air, it makes use of a massive quantity of gasoline to generate strength and launch itself into the sky, but, while it's miles up there, the gasoline to keep itself is an entire lot much less. The same component takes location with our mind! To trade an ingrained addiction, you need a variety of power to encompass it into your gadget and make it computerized.

Now, I'm going to say a few factor as a manner to shock you: this large expenditure of power is to execute this new dependancy, but, focusing on bodily interest, you need to begin this new addiction slowly and frequently.

How it definitely works, normally the large majority of humans start something with the highest gas, however all this fuel empties brief, this is because of the fact their tool has no longer included that sample. Therefore, the man or woman desires to take a look at all this gas, but in a focused and sensible manner.

For example, a person who begins training at the health club and desires to start doing 15 machines and placing on the whole load they may be in a role to attend to, desires to do as masses as they're able to that day, that week. However, the massive hassle is that your mind desires to hold energy, so, in your thoughts, you'll a race in competition to death, so it's going to try everything to discourage you from returning and, inside the large majority, it wins.

The right trouble to do is to pay attention all this power of will in a greater focused way, performing the physical sports extra gently, setting durations of variant into your training and little by little growing the weight. This whole tool permits you get your mind used to this new addiction, incorporating it into your habitual; So, within the long term, as you repeat the method plenty it turns into computerized and grow to be part of your lifestyles.

However, humans make errors sooner or later of the variation period, they need to position into effect a brand new addiction as although it have been already a part of their lifestyles, but that is not how the thoughts works. Your mind wants to create what we name a neural trail and improve it, so this may turn out to be a part of your life.

The Achilles heel of bad conduct is that their praise is on the spot, that is, you bought it right now; and the reward of correct conduct comes over a long term, so your mind sabotages you, that is why I'm displaying you the importance of knowledge precisely what you need and now not getting discouraged through way of the get rid of of some effects, now not giving up, know-how that the time spoon will arrive.

Chapter 12: Of the Solutions

We input this international with now not a few thing however existence and we do not know while we will skip, so, in brief, we do no longer non-public a few factor, no longer even our very very personal life. Even so, we act as though we were the proprietors of purpose, but the splendid reality is that we take into account in things that during fact are not anything extra than a mere sensory notion and the large troubles in life are in reality increased perceptions. What seems large to us is actually now not that large. In this enjoy, there may be a word that declares: "Will some thing that looks as if a huge trouble these days even though be a big hassle in 5 years?" If the solution is advantageous, then clearly fear, the massive issue is that the overpowering majority of the time the answer is not any.

The reality is that nobody is aware of all the solutions and in no way will, existence is handiest for us to accumulate excellent moments, critiques and stories.

I truly just like the following tale as it destroys the notion of folks who assume that it's far simplest cash and numerous energy that deliver happiness, and others who remember that being terrible is honorable, however neither of the 2 states brings real happiness, as that could be a internal state, a real intellectual alchemy.

In Ancient India, there was a completely wealthy and powerful king who had a son named Siddhartha Gautama. This king promised that his son could probably in no manner recognize ache and struggling in existence. When the little prince come to be born, he raised all of the castle partitions and ordered that the prince should in no way depart the fort walls. From his begin, the king gave the whole thing to Siddhartha, the little prince grew up having the high-quality and the outstanding, however indoors his heart he felt a awesome emptiness that he did not recognise the way to offer an motive of.

One day, he asked a servant to take him past the fort walls. Thus, he come to be hidden, and at the same time as he observed the reality, he grow to be stunned. There he noticed human beings's poverty, fear and ache. Feeling indignant, he blamed his father for by no means displaying him that truth, it virtually is why he felt that emptiness. Siddhartha determined it became time to transport looking for his fact and fill his vacancy, and he did so. He left the castle and abdicated his throne.

Spending years in poverty, hunger and cold, he got here to the conclusion that there has been no the Aristocracy in poverty, as he endured with the identical vacancy in his heart. Determined to recognise his fact, he spent years on religious searches. One day, he determined to meditate below a fig tree and could handiest depart there after discovering the which means of existence. He contemplated for 7 weeks (40 9 days), resisting fears and temptations, and on the 40 ninth day he had spiritual enlightenment and at that 2d he knew the meaning of lifestyles. Regarding this, he explains that he's neither in riches nor in poverty, as each the wealthy and the terrible undergo; real wealth is, consequently, within the hearts of fellows.

This man was BUDDHA, and from that day on he dedicated his existence to education people and supporting the maximum humble.

Here are a few education that this man left us for us to understand and, if it makes revel in, observe:

Even when you have a have a look at loads of sacred scriptures or even in case you speak about them lots, what accurate can they do for you in case you do not act on it?

The way isn't always within the sky, the manner is inside the coronary heart.

A jug fills drop via way of drop.

Every individual is the author of their non-public health or their very own contamination.

To understand the whole thing you need to forgive the whole thing.

Better than one thousand empty phrases is a word that brings peace.

Any phrases we utter must be decided on carefully, due to the fact human beings listen them and are advocated by using manner of them, for better or worse.

No one saves us but ourselves, nobody can and no man or woman succeeds. We want to stroll the route ourselves.

At the time of a problem at the same time as we feel angry, we save you preventing for the fact and start preventing with ourselves.

In heaven, there can be no distinction among East and West; humans create variations inner their very very own minds and then trust them to be proper.

Those who're loose from spiteful thoughts honestly discover peace.

Hatred does now not prevent with hatred at any time, hatred ceases with love. This is an unchangeable regulation.

There ought to be evil so that correct can display its purity above it.

It is simple to appearance the faults of others, however it is tough to see our very personal faults. He who suggests the defects of others is like someone who throws straw to the wind, but covers up his very very own flaws like a cunning gambler at the same time as he hides his statistics.

I in no way see what has been carried out; I best see what remains to be finished.

The thoughts is everything: what you agree with you studied, you come to be.

Just as treasures are determined from the earth, high-quality feature seems in right deeds, and expertise seems from a herbal and peaceful thoughts. To walk very well via the labyrinth of human existence, one wishes the moderate of knowledge and the guidance of virtue.

We are normal via our thoughts; we come to be what we count on. When the thoughts is natural, delight follows like a shadow that in no way is going away.

Work to your non-public salvation. Don't depend upon others.

Let's upward thrust up and be thankful, because of the reality if we didn't research masses nowadays, at least we determined out a bit, and if we did no longer study a touch, at the least we did not get unwell, and if we have been given sick, at the least we did no longer die; So, allow's all be grateful.

You can't stroll the course till you end up the path itself.

You will now not be punished for your anger, you'll be punished for your anger.

Conquering your self is a more venture than conquering others.

Three subjects can not be hidden for lengthy: the solar, the moon and the truth.

Have compassion for all beings, rich and poor; each person has their private suffering. Some undergo too much, others too little.

Today, I observed some thing that absolutely caught my hobby. I became watching a sequence for mastering features, but the plot captivated me a lot that I absolutely commenced to similar to the collection. The tale takes location inside the mid-nineteenth century and revolves around a vampire, who, because the plot unfolds, sleeps and wakes up in the contemporary. In one of the scenes, he surely stops at a exquisite residence so he can take blood and eventually finally ends up having a protracted communication approximately dramaturgy alongside together together with his victim. Then, this vampire admires the fixtures in his victim's residence and says:

I actually have lived in glory and wealth all my lifestyles and I actually have in no manner visible such wealth. Kings and monarchs in no way dreamed of getting the entirety you've got were given, they might give everything, castles, riches, to have all of it.

This speech caught my interest and made me reflect masses, see how interesting it is: in recent times, no matter how terrible someone is, they have got power at home, a cellular cellular telephone, variety, color TV, laptop, some form of transport …Now have a look at that, in principle, she lives higher than any king within the Middle Ages lived, as she has subjects that no royalty ever dreamed of possessing and will supply anything in lifestyles to have. Despite having such a lot of "modern" things, humans are not glad and in no way could be, due to the truth, as I cited above, happiness is a intellectual state, it is accepting what you have got were given at that 2d, taking care of it with all the care and affection.

We people are familiar with everything fabric. When you gain a few detail, there may be satisfaction, but, because the days move with the aid of using, it turns into so blanketed into your routine and device that it will become some issue normal. Maybe seeing a person the usage of a Ferrari looks as if a few component from a few different planet to you, but for that man or woman it's far a few factor normal, genuinely every exceptional day riding to paintings.

When I have become a teenager, I appeared forward to turning 18. For me, undertaking that age is probably a first-rate change, it'd be like exploring a brand new worldwide. My dad and mom had been continuously strict in my upbringing approximately being able to go out, I felt trapped, I needed to stay at domestic or close by, at a wonderful time my mom might check me.

So, after I grew to become 18, I fell into the world, ventured out, went attempting to find what I constantly favored. My mother, alas, suffered, but I located that I did not definitely come to be free once I have become 18 (at the least not the concept of freedom that I had conceived). I received masses greater duties and masses extra responsibilities, I needed to learn how to cope and determine to myself, it is the tough fact of the region. Now I had another form of mission, I desired to be a person in lifestyles, to be reliable, to have coins, to tour hundreds… These had been some of my goals in lifestyles.

When I went to university, I failed to need to sit down at the back of a chair, it wasn't my profile, I'm communicative and kinesthetic, I needed to get my fingers grimy. Imagine what occurred. I come to be the king of the hallway, going to elegance killed me, I did not experience like I have turn out to be in my "habitat"; In truth, I could not take in something, instructions had been darkness for me, however I had the subsequent idea: after I graduate, I is probably free, just like when I became 18, I need to have my independence, human beings will understand me, I may have my venture of Dreams.

You need to understand how an entire lot electricity is spent on university. It's four, five, 6 years of have a observe and economic investment in frequently some thing you do not even like, all of this and then you can not even get a task that suits your career or will pay you a bit greater than the minimum salary. Then you find out, after this adventure, that you won't be happy due to the truth you finished college, that that is genuinely some other small a part of your journey. I do now not need to belittle people who go to college, in truth I assume it's miles very crucial to examine, but I great assume it's far essential to go to college if your chosen profession requires one; don't visit university to say you likely did it or because your mother and father want that aspect for you.

Unfortunately, the economic technology has indoctrinated a whole lot of humans, and people definitely receive as proper with that going to college or getting accurate grades is synonymous with achievement, you need to deconstruct this proper away, as it's not right, what makes you a success is being self-taught and having energy of motion, perform.

From a younger age at university, they need us to memorize numerous content material fabric cloth that we will in no way use in our lives, but they fail to teach the requirements, together with: non-public budget, emotion control, first aid, manage, nutrients, entrepreneurship, creativity, innovation, problem fixing and so forth, an countless range of things...

Someone is interested by this modern version, however you, who are now a logician, as short as you've got got children, recollect complementary education to train your baby to suppose with every hemispheres of the thoughts, so that he moreover becomes a reality seeker and no longer a in the middle of the herd.

What this model highlights is which you want to beautify topics. For starters, it does now not show you that your mind works using elements (proper and left mind). I'll located a few other model underneath to offer an motive at the back of it more really:

There are youngsters who use the right component extra constantly and others the left aspect, but everybody want to learn how to use every components. However, that is genuinely one aspect on this complete chain of mistakes, children are expert to memorize formula and things to get properly grades, when they develop up they go to university, which usually would not have masses to do with their abilities and dreams, they pick out out some aspect that offers extra cash, or a few factor their mother and father need them to do, and after years of software program, the day comes that they graduate and start their conflict for artwork. Then comes the lots-preferred approach, and there they begin their adventure, however they'll be faced with many conflicts, as the college taught them the technical issue, but not some thing about management, relationships, trouble fixing, manipulate and masses of other subjects, to stand out in their professions.

Thus, many stay in corporations for years, stagnant, with out the slightest choice to boom and increase; the giant majority carry the burden of exertions, as they hate what they do, however they have commitments and households to assist and dream of the day they may retire for you to enjoy life.

Well, time passes and the big day in their retirement arrives, so those humans acquire a earnings that barely will pay the bills and now they have got an entire lot of time, however they recognise that they don't have sufficient electricity or cash to experience lifestyles. Then frustration starts offevolved offevolved offevolved knocking at the door.

This version is replicated via tens of hundreds of thousands and tens of thousands and thousands of humans as the right version, however we want to deconstruct this. You and I honestly have an obligation to open our mouths and alternate this and the subsequent generations!

Can you be aware the distinction?

165

This version may be carried out little by little, the populace is probably grade by grade transformed. With all of the technology at our disposal, no matter how a good buy you want to shut your eyes to this fact, it's going to enter your thoughts so strongly that now not some issue may be able to take it away! The outcome of this contemporary-day version is the era of consumerism.

Generation of consumerism

Not that that may be a problem in itself, we want to eat food, garments, gadgets, however there may be a difference among eating and overspending, exaggerating, shopping for out of compulsion. Many humans are so pissed off with life and the model they agree to that they take out all this emotional waste in buying and extra buying, which ends up becoming a pile of things of their lives.

Companies and businesses understand this very well and take the possibility to apply it in the direction of you and sell your emotion.

Surely while you switch in your TV, advertising and marketing will pop up at the display display and demand that you purchase a few component. Now you try to trade the scene, choose out up your mobile mobile phone to look some issue on a social network and there are many greater advertisements, announcing: purchase this, buy that, "on the way to have a better existence, you want this product, it'll revolutionize lifestyles. Your life!". You go with the flow to take a look at a video on YouTube to look at something and it's far whole of commercials. The international around us is continuously making us want subjects to shop for. "Look at this new mobile cellular telephone, it has a certainly new feature so one can make your pix appear like experts", and so forth, it in no way stops... Our society is capitalist, and there's no hassle the least bit at this component, this is the game and we should play, but my factor is that you cannot be taken over through fickle impulses, over excited via feelings, or primarily based on celebrities.

Do you need to peer how certainly elegant and influenceable the area is? Once, the participant Ronaldo "Fenômeno", within the 2002 World Cup, launched a fashion that became a horrible haircut, he shaved his whole head and left excellent a chunk hair inside the the front, just like the person Cascão from Turma da Mônica, and it have become a rage, all the youngsters had that haircut. The query is: why? Simple, a determine of strength, the instance you have. We will always be stimulated, however we should realize by means of whom and while, we need to dominate, now not allow models or manufacturers have an impact on us to spend or do matters out of herbal emotion. It's difficult, however no longer not viable.

There is a commercial agency known as neuromarketing, that may be a observe that delves into expertise the thoughts and feelings to discover ways to sell to your thoughts.

Your thoughts is separated into three additives:

Reptilian thoughts: Brain responsible for options that cause survival. As it's miles the oldest a part of the mind, it consists of all instinctive emotions, for example: ache, starvation, reflexes, respiration, power or maybe violence as a method of survival.

Chapter 13: Nature Must Be Decided

Einstein have become right, we ought to observe nature, now not great due to the fact it's miles lovable (it is also why), but heaps greater than that, because of its ability for replica and abundance. If you do no longer realize, I want to inform you, you are a part of nature, however most of the time you do now not understand it. Nature has two very weird subjects: the seed and abundance; To exhibit this, I will use the orange tree analogy, but you may observe this in any form of tree.

The orange tree has a natural duty to supply definitely one orange, as its number one function in nature is to breed and, to fulfill this feature, it produces many, many oranges; there are countless seeds, some of the equal ones. But why all this abundance? Because the Universe is widespread, certainly as nature is sufficient and you and I are ok, however some issue happened in our lives that blocked us, clearly so we started to consider that we need to simply accept little and stay with little. However, that is unnatural, we're living contrary to what we were born to be.

The first aspect that makes us like this is the truth that we do not apprehend a way to use the seeds we've. And what are our seeds? Dear reader, our seeds are our ideas, we've got were given were given the ones seeds in reality, however we want to recognize a way to plant them; That's wherein people fail, they do not apprehend the way to plant, inside the event that they knew they will multiply the fruits loads of instances. I'll provide you with an example: if you plant a corn seed, that corn plant can be able to produce 2 ears with spherical 500 seeds every; So, in case you harvest and replant, how many seeds will you have got were given?

When you learn how to plant, no person will stop your multiplication, you may be like a river that flows into the sea. And the manner to plant those seeds? First, you need to have a totally strong and clean reason, it truly is why I asked you to explain it at the begin. Maybe you are thinking in case you want to have cash to plant, then you definately simply are wrong, you may want a splendid seed, or the "concept", then a network, that is one of the massive keys, then you may need to apprehend a way to sell, you can moreover want remedy troubles and lead humans. With the ones attributes, you could now start sowing loads of seeds within the route of your harvests, with a view to no longer be few.

It looks as if a totally smooth systematization to carry out, and actually it's miles in fact easy, however the massive majority of humans are not knowledgeable and disciplined to look at this model, they do no longer recognize the manner to community, they expect they have to first-class have their general pals and that is it. High-tremendous; The person desires to get to the desk of any eating place and boast about their achievements, inflating their ego like a blowfish with out getting to know something and with out taking note of any actual tale.

The good sized majority of humans think that in reality going for walks hard will make the whole thing exercising session. My reader pal, I'm improper, so that you can reap fulfillment, eighty 5% of it relies upon to your community, that is, your relationships. Look at the bricklayer, now not belittling the career, of route, however as an entire, bricklayers paintings tough all their lives and do not get a whole lot greater than a house to live in. Of path, the ones who've a unique mentality speedy stand out of their area and are able to installation a industrial organization enterprise, developing and growing thanks to their capacity to narrate and hold relationships.

A certain guy commenced selling luxurious boats and every morning he may additionally need to located on his running garments, his favorite yellow shoes and opt for a run within the marina. There, he commenced out to make buddies with the regulars and talk approximately the boats leaning closer to the pier, with out bringing up that he have become a deliver salesman, and made an amazing discovery: most boat owners rarely rode in them, and he additionally located that they frequented a tennis membership inside the region. This man, very astute, joined the tennis membership and began out his adventure as a tennis player, each day he done and made buddies with the guys who attended there, and, after a while, the humans, due to the fact they favored him and their right arrogance, they constantly requested:

What's your profession?

He usually answered:

I sell luxurious boats.

These very influential men stated that they had one or buddies who desired to shop for a supply, but did not recognize wherein to discover one, so the vendor gently passed them a card and asked them to name him, and that manner he provided boats at the same time as now not having to exit presenting boats. .

Can you be aware the electricity of the network?

How to build robust networks?

No one will ever make pinnacle nets in a 180º function, it desires to be vertical, at a 90º attitude.

It is vital to move. First step, decide your situation of interest, look for a success human beings in that trouble, studies them, find out which places they commonplace, pick out out close to pals, find out in which they journey and what their preferred sports sports are. Take a real have a study your conduct and customs, then begin going to these places and make friends with everybody you may who will let you to your technique. As you infiltrate this new worldwide, doors will open for you. A incredible location to network are education and development publications to your area of interest, so on every occasion you take detail within the ones events, speak to each person, mingle, pay hobby, and most significantly, get contacts, this manner your network will increase and masses of doorways will open.

Know a manner to sell

There are people who tremble at the lowest while this term is mentioned, they've got traumas and blocks regarding earnings, however the superb truth is that they'll be promoting all of the time. When they want to exit and their partner does no longer need to move, they create (sell) arguments to persuade; via going to their jobs and staying there for eight hours a day, they will be selling their time; whilst going for a method interview, they're selling their photo and records; after they go to a party and flirt with a woman, they're promoting their persona. So, expensive reader, you are constantly promoting! But people take this term within the following connotation:

In most people's minds, income are formatted this way, in order that they take shipping of that the company is to stay the manner they may be and stay caught in paintings for the relaxation of their lives. What they don't know is that the best sowers on planet Earth are amazing salespeople, the richest men in the world apprehend a way to sell. As my father would possibly say: "I even sell molten lead".

However, proper salespeople get right of entry to inconceivable riches, subjects that first-class they are capable of collect, because in case you do now not learn how to promote, you will be doomed to failure; the technique is straightforward: without earnings there is no wealth, therefore, you'll be a slave.

When you get proper of get admission to to this diploma of attention, a key will flip for your mind and you may flow into directly to some specific stage, this is one of the maximum essential competencies you want in your existence. If you have got tremendous problem in earnings, you urgently want to take a few courses to end up a higher shop clerk, as promoting is an art work, and much more complex than it seems.

Chapter 14: The Biggest Asset You Personal

I undergo in mind once I turn out to be more youthful and studied in high university, teachers need to supply art work in companies and we would have to gift those works to the whole beauty. That comes to be the give up for me. Firstly, in any pastime, some have been devoted and others determined fit. I moreover recollect that topics were worrying, I become ridiculous at it, my displays were horrible, I stuttered, my legs shook, I stated the entirety wrong. I maintain in thoughts a particular episode wherein I became all devoted to art work, domestic made cardboard, hard but normal speech, sweat on each part of my face and frame, but there I end up, corporation and robust, I couldn't take a look at all people , only for the female I even have emerge as in love with, she appeared to be taking component in the presentation, as she seemed attentively, however my sadness turn out to be brief and exceptional, because of the reality once I finished the presentation she regarded with the ones large, deep eyes and said: "I didn't understand a few detail about it. That spoke". Damn, it finished me off, I sweated and shook even extra, I did now not apprehend what to do and the trainer even tons less so, the entire elegance burst into laughter and I left embarrassed and went again to my desk.

Thousands of teens and kids go through comparable episodes and masses of emerge as growing emotional blocks so strong that they could not even have a study nicely as adults, others can't even gift themselves to a bigger wide style of humans, I do not blame anyone, however I say that the lack of coaching The school and instructors are superb.

The focus of these shows ought to now not even be on whether or not the scholars understood the content, however alternatively on turning into suitable at public speaking and putting off the difficulties of presenting themselves to the overall public, just so children increase up greater prepared for the future and might take their ideas to the general public. As many humans as viable.

Because of those and precise episodes, young people create the mentality of in no manner analyzing over again, that reading is horrible, that studying is silly; I emerge as like that myself, I recall that I surely regarded beforehand to the quantity in my lifestyles wherein I may graduate, after which in no manner take a look at all over again.

I don't forget that maximum humans assume this way, not that it is their fault, but I suppose there's an excessive amount of stress, society shapes us, we are programmed to have a observe this pattern in the call of "fulfillment" and below penalty of "failure"; It's as even though we had been robots and society was our programmer.

Luckily for me, I turn out to be continuously very curious and tried to recognize the entirety that occurred to me and how I might also want to emerge as someone better; So, I rejected what was "programmed" for me. There was a few aspect specific along the manner that modified everything in my existence, I will supply an cause of this later.

Once, in 2017, I modified into at the airport geared up for some different revel in and I had to spend hours and hours in one of the flight connections, my handiest opportunity changed into to visit a nearby book vicinity and purchase a ebook, remembering that I continuously had I had this addiction of purchasing books once I traveled, but the shame changed into that I almost by no means look at them. But that day have emerge as special, it hit me with pain, due to the fact I determined out that I usually do away with studying my books. Are books actually an airport pastime?